Profitable No-Load Mutual Fund Trading Techniques For The Individual Investor

Profitable No-Load Mutual Fund Trading Techniques

For The Individual Investor

by Norman Mallory

Windsor Books, Brightwaters, New York

Published by Windsor Books
P.O. Box 280
Brightwaters, N.Y., 11718

Manufatured in the United States of America

ISBN 0-930233-11-5

TABLE OF CONTENTS

PART I   THE STOCK MARKET

PART II   THE GOLD MARKET

PART III   THE BOND MARKET

APPENDICES

PREFACE

The way to make money trading in the markets is simply to become fully invested in good performing no-load mutual funds very early in bull markets and to conserve capital during bear markets. The system presented in this book will teach you how to do just that.

There is no argument that if investments in the stock, bond, or gold markets were limited only to their bull segments, fantastic gains would be realized. These could then be protected in cash havens during bear markets. Of course, the trick is to be able to identify the bull when it arrives. Perhaps you have heard the expression, "they don't ring a bell when the bull market begins." If bull and bear markets could be identified, who would be invested during bear markets? Obviously, all investors expect to make a profit from their investments, otherwise they would keep their money in the bank. In reality, most investors do not know that a bull market has started for sure until a large part of the move is over—then they are afraid to buy into the market because it is too high. Eventually, they become really convinced as the bull market persists and they hear and read how others are making so much money. Now they make their purchases—just as the bull move has ended. Witness the spring of 1983, near the end of the great 1982-1983 bull market. Mutual fund sales rose to new all time records as redemptions dried up. The end was now in sight.

The market peaked in June, as the professionals relentlessly distributed their overpriced shares by way of mutual funds to new investors just entering the market.

Similarly, these new investors, as well as the old, do not know that the bear market has started until disastrous losses have been forced upon them. Why will investors never learn not to enter the market right at the top? It is the nature of the bull and the bear to confound the investor, especially the novice, so that predicting the future course of the market with any degree of accuracy becomes almost an impossibility.

It is difficult to define bull and bear markets even after the fact. During the course of a bull market, there may be several sharp declines, followed by rallies that take the market to new highs. In bear markets, there often are sharp rallies that may be mistaken for the beginning of a new bull market. A bull market cannot be defined by the minimum advance it must achieve or by the length of time it must last. When bull markets start, the economy is usually deep in recession, confidence in the future is at a low point, the current market decline is expected to continue, and the last thing that investors want to do is commit money to the market. Conversely, when bear markets begin, the economy is generally at a high point, business is booming and it appears that the market will go up forever.

It was precisely because of these difficulties that I spent the past several years developing an investment program that would not depend upon prediction of the future course of the market. The system is relatively simple, so novice investors can participate. It requires a minimum of time because most investors are working for a living and have precious little time to devote to the markets. Trading is kept to a minimum. Finally, the rewards greatly outweigh the risks, so the system has very high profit expectations. The strategy for the development of the system was fairly simple—study the past history of the markets and determine whether a trend-following approach, a cyclical approach, or a combination of these will most likely give satisfactory results in the future.

I studied the movement of the New York Stock Exchange prices over a 20 year period, from 1964 through 1984. With only a few exceptions, the market was found to be cyclical. A system was devised that stresses the accumulation of equity mutual funds near the bottom of a cycle and the sale of them somewhere near the top. The method has been very successful, as will be seen later on.

The six year period between 1978 and 1984 was used as a test period for the stock market system. Net asset value data was obtained for a number of equity mutual funds. This data was used to duplicate the purchase and sale of shares while strictly following the buy and sell signals as they were developed by the system. Two fine bull markets for stocks produced excellent profits. The first one got underway in March of 1980 and the second one started in August of 1982. The latter one carried the market to new all time highs and did not peak out until late in June, 1983. On five other occasions, there were sharp rallies that may have been mistaken for the start of new bull markets, but all proved to be false starts. The trading system also carried us safely through the long bear market of 1981-1982.

The gold share market was studied in a similar fashion, beginning in 1974. The net asset value of the United Services Gold Shares Fund was used as a price index. Despite the general consensus that gold shares should be traded only with a trend-following approach, I have had much better success with a combined trend-following and cyclical approach. Again, accumulating shares near the bottom of a cycle and selling out near the top.

The market for gold stocks was almost perfectly flat during all of 1978. It then took an upward turn in 1979, gathered great upward momentum during 1980 and finally reached its peak in September of that year, as the price of gold rose above $800 an ounce! The bear market that followed lasted almost two years, finally bottoming out in June of 1982 with the price of gold back down to $300 an ounce. A new bull market then got started and carried well into 1983. Since then, the market has been erratic, with sharp rallies and declines.

Bonds can be traded very successfully with a trend-following system. The price movement of bonds was studied in detail since 1979. It was found that bonds have been an excellent and rewarding low-risk trading vehicle. I firmly believe that all investors should be switching between bonds and money market funds using this relatively simple system to increase both their income and their capital.

Bond prices have not been kind to long term investors. The market was in a bear phase all through 1978 and 1979, terminating with a sharp sell-off that ended in April of 1980. The following rally was brief, and the downtrend continued without letting up until February of 1982 when the final double bottom was made. A bull market started in July of that year and lasted until the end of May, 1983 and proved to be the finest bond market rally in years. A bear market then set in, lasted a year and took back a good portion of the gains. A new bull market began in July of 1984.

No-load mutual funds were selected as the trading medium for the three market areas for many reasons, which will be presented and discussed later. Among these reasons are easy selection, immediate diversification, no commissions and telephone purchase and exchange privileges.

After an introduction to no-load mutual funds, in the first part of this book, we will develop the system for trading in the stock market using equity no-load mutual funds. The next section teaches the system for trading the United Services Gold Shares Fund. Finally, the last part will present a system for trading bond mutual funds.

MUTUAL FUNDS

In order to make the trading system work properly, it is essential to invest in a portfolio of stocks or bonds that is widely diversified. This is necessary to insure that the value of the entire portfolio will move in the same direction as the market.

As suggested earlier, it is highly recommended that investments by novice or non-expert investors be limited to no-load mutual funds. While an investor skilled in the art of evaluation and selection procedures may readily assemble a diversified portfolio of stocks or bonds, this would be a formidable task for most people. The mere fact that there are thousands of stocks and bonds listed on the exchanges will overwhelm the average person. Of course, there are also hundreds of mutual funds listed in the daily papers. But the selection of suitable funds for trading the systems will not be too difficult.

In addition to the minimum amount of time required for the selection of a stock or bond fund, mutual funds have many other advantages over individual common stocks and bonds. Some of these are:

1. Regardless of how small the investment, it is spread equally over the mutual fund's entire portfolio, thus achieving instant diversification.

2. No-load funds do not charge the investor any commissions to buy or sell shares of the fund.

3. All mutual funds provide professional management of the fund's portfolio.

4. Mutual funds trade relatively large blocks of stock in each transaction. This keeps the commissions paid by the funds to their brokers at a minimum and helps to keep management expenses down.

5. Most growth-oriented equity mutual funds track the market very closely. The available time of the investor can be given to the timing of purchases and sales rather than to stock selection.

6. During a bull market, many well managed equity growth funds will outperform the market to the upside by a wide margin.

7. Investors can take advantage of the higher yielding bond funds, since the diversification and professional management of these lower quality funds essentially reduces the risk to minimal levels.

Obviously, mutual funds must charge a fee for their management services. Most often, the annual fee is approximately 1% or less of the money which they manage. Usually, this fee is removed from the assets of the fund on a monthly basis and the investor is not even aware that he is paying the fee. One must read the prospectus of the fund to determine the fee schedule. Considering the services offered by the funds and the advantages of mutual fund investing, these modest fees are usually an excellent bargain.

Management fees are often confused with sales charges imposed by load funds. It should be well understood that all mutual funds, load and no-load alike, charge management fees, while only the load funds charge commissions to buy or sell shares of the fund. The sales commission serves no purpose for an investor—it is simply given to the salesman or broker who happens to sell shares of the fund to a customer. Sales charges are often about 8.5%, which means that if you invested $10,000 in a fund, $850 would be given to the broker and the remaining $9,150 would be invested in the fund for you. The fund will now have to gain 9% due to appreciation in order for the investor just to get even. In a no-load fund, the full $10,000 would be invested directly into shares of the fund. Today, a majority of mutual fund investors are taking advantage of the no-load feature. To save the considerable commissions and open a no-load mutual fund account, you have to avoid the brokers and contact the fund directly in order to invest. Mutual funds have been making this chore easier by offering toll-free telephone numbers. Potential investors can contact the fund and obtain a prospectus without writing a letter or paying for a telephone call. To take advantage of no-load investing today, one needs only to obtain the appropriate telephone numbers. An excellent no-load fund directory may be obtained by sending $2.00 to:

No-Load Mutual Fund Association, Inc.
11 Penn Plaza, Suite 2204
New York, NY 10017

While this booklet is strictly a directory and does not make recommendations or give performance comparisons, it does give essential information on the individual funds, including investment objectives and whether or not the fund permits telephone exchanges or telephone purchases. Many types of funds are listed, including bond funds and money market funds.

A more complete source of information on mutual funds is the Barron's weekly financial publication. About six weeks after the end of each quarter, Barron's publishes a feature on mutual funds which includes timely articles on the best performing funds. Tabulated data is given for each mutual fund, load or no-load, to show its performance over the last one year and last five years. Forbes magazine publishes a special mutual fund edition each August. Their unique performance rating system is applied to all funds that have a five year history. These special editions of Forbes are an excellent source of information for fund investors. One will also find many advertisements for mutual fund advisory services in Barron's and Forbes. Most of these will offer an introductory trial subscription or a sample copy for a minimal cost. With one or two of these trial copies, you can quickly find out about some of the best performing funds.

Selection of a mutual fund for investing in bonds will not be a problem. Bond funds are chosen from one of three categories—government bonds, corporate bonds, or high yield corporate bonds. The high yield, lower quality corporate bond funds are preferred, since there is no reason why a professionally managed portfolio of lower quality bonds should entail any serious risk to the investor. However, if you don't feel secure with the high yield bonds, regular high quality corporate or government bond funds are readily available. Many families of mutual funds offer one or more of these bond funds, as well as the telephone switching privilege between bond funds and their money market funds.

The only gold mining fund to be considered at the present time is the United Services Gold Shares fund. This fund has been in operation since 1974 and therefore has a suitable history. The historical price data for the U.S. Gold Shares fund was used for the development of the trading system. New gold funds are coming to market more frequently and will probably be suitable for investing once they become established and have price histories of about five years. It is still questionable whether the buy and sell signals developed on the United Services fund will be applicable to other gold funds with as much success.

The greatest difficulty in fund selection will be associated with the stock funds, simply because there are so many to choose from. Newer investors may handle this problem by selecting just one or two fund families in order to get started. A fund family is one which offers several equity mutual funds, each with different investment objectives, one or more bond funds and at least one money market fund. Nearly all fund families now permit telephone exchanges between the various funds, although there may be some restrictions on frequency of trading. As the investor becomes more experienced, it is a simple matter to start the next market cycle with a new fund family.

As will be discussed later, there may be times when market

leadership will direct investments into a higher quality fund rather than an aggressive growth fund. A family of funds will usually have one available. For example, the Boston family of funds includes the following: the Capital Appreciation Fund, which is a high quality stock fund; the Special Growth Fund, which is a more aggressive stock fund; the Managed Income Fund, which is a high quality bond fund; and the Cash Management Fund, which is a money market fund. At present, there are no restrictions on toll-free telephone exchanges between funds and there are no charges to the investor when an exchange is made. Management fees for the four funds range between ½% and 1% of assets under management.

Another innovation introduced by some mutual funds in recent years is to permit existing shareholders to make purchases by telephone. If you already have an account with the fund, a purchase may be made by calling the fund, giving your account number and indicating the dollar amount of the purchase. Shares will be bought in that amount at the day's closing price for that fund. The purchase will be honored as long as the fund receives a check within seven days. This mechanism is very useful for a system that involves a series of purchases, such as the one you're about to learn in this book. It permits the inclusion of some very excellent performing funds in the system. It should be understood that funds which permit telephone purchases do not allow telephone redemptions. If telephone exchanges are also not permitted, an overnight letter service will have to be used to expedite fund sales. The United Services Gold Shares Fund permits telephone purchases as well as telephone exchanges.

A final word about telephone exchanges. The investor should be careful to learn about any restrictions associated with these exchanges. For example, the T. Rowe Price funds require a wait of 90 days before a round trip exchange may be completed. The Stein Roe group permits four round trip exchanges per year. The Scudder funds warn that exchanges for the purpose of short term trading are not permitted, but give no further definition of short term. Vanguard does not permit telephone exchanges between all of its funds, with the popular Explorer Fund being one of the excluded funds. Fidelity permits four round trip exchanges per year, which seems adequate. Additional exchanges may be made for a fee of $50. An investor should be prepared to adapt to these restrictions if one of these fund families is selected. All of the funds will accept written instructions for redemptions at any time if the signatures are properly guaranteed by a commercial bank or brokerage firm.

Part I
THE STOCK MARKET

Introduction

If it is granted that equity no-load mutual funds are the best investment for most investors, how should one go about taking a position in the market? All mutual fund managements will suggest a program such as this:

1. Define your investment objectives and select a suitable fund.
2. Accumulate shares continuously as more capital becomes available.
3. Hold the shares through all market cycles, including bear markets. Rely on the fund management to limit bear market losses.
4. Switch to a different fund only when your investment objectives change.

This would be sound advice if the stock market had a continual upward bias. Investors would commit their capital and watch it grow. New capital could be added with confidence. But that's not the case. New investors are likely to enter the market near the top of a long bull move. This is when the success stories about investing receive the most publicity and advertising budgets are at their peaks. The expectant investor has finally been convinced that easy profits are available. Brokers and money managers are proclaiming that the "next leg" of the bull market is about to begin.

Mutual fund sales to investors will rise to record levels near the end of a bull market. This only means that a new record number of investors will suffer heavy losses in the following bear market. New investors taking positions during the 1968-1969 "go-go" years suffered devastating losses by 1975. They left the market and didn't return until late 1980, just in time for the 1981-1982 bear market. They came back in new record numbers in early 1983, only to suffer losses through 1984. Now, with the market at record highs, mutual fund sales are also at record highs. One only wonders what the future will bring.

Suppose we reverse this procedure. Let's try to buy into mutual funds during, or even better, near the bottom of a bear market. Also, let's not plan to hold our shares through all market cycles, but only until the next bull market is coming to an end. Then let's put our capital into money market funds, safely awaiting the end of the next bear market. Timing is everything!

To reap the really big profits from the stock market, it is absolutely essential to become fully invested very early in a new bull market and to sell out somewhere near the final high point. It is most difficult, if not impossible, to take substantial profits from bear market rallies or from markets that are flat. Unfortunately, bull markets come along only rarely, perhaps once every three or four years. When they do come, we must invest near the beginning of the upmove. Therefore, it is our intention to devise a plan to do just that.

The trading system is designed to take advantage of intermediate term market cycles, as defined by the movements of the New York Stock Exchange (NYSE) Index. The system demands both patience and discipline, but with only a light work load somewhat tailored to the individual's desire to increase his profits. Buy and sell signals are automatic and must be acted upon on the day they are received. Profit expectations are very high and are generated primarily from the bull markets that are encountered. From the other market cycles, we expect only minor profits or perhaps even small losses. The risk of a severe loss is minimal, since we have a mechanism to take us out of the market if it should turn against us. No-load equity mutual funds that accept telephone purchases are the mandatory trading vehicles. Those that permit exchanges between funds by means of a telephone call are preferred.

What kind of results do we expect from the system? Using the net asset value (NAV) data for the Constellation Growth Fund, and acting on each buy and sell signal as developed by the system, $10,000 would have grown to $50,730 during the six year test period between 1978 and 1985. This profit of 407% is equivalent to an annual compounded return of 31.1%. Several other no-load funds for which data is available also gave very satisfactory results. For example, the Stein Roe Capital Opportunities Fund grew to $40,500 for a compounded annual return of 26.3%. These results assume the reinvestment of all dividends, capital gain distributions and trading profits, but do not include any interest from money market funds. If money market interest were included at rates equivalent to 91-day Treasury Bills, the Constellation fund investment would have appreciated to $63,300 in the six year period, for a compounded return of 35.7% per year. It is fair to consider the money market interest, because our capital was invested in the equity funds for only about two-thirds of the time and in money market funds for about one-third of the time —a significant ratio.

MARKET TRADING CYCLES

The New York Stock Exchange Composite Index is a capitalization-weighted index that includes every common stock traded on the exchange. As such, it adequately measures the movement of the stock market as a whole, since it is not limited to just the 30 large companies in the Dow Jones Industrial Index or the 500 stocks that make up the Standard & Poor's Index. For this reason, the NYSE Index was chosen as the price index to measure the movement of the stock market to show results of the trading system.

The NYSE Index has been published on a daily basis since May 28, 1964. The daily values of the index have been plotted on graphs and are included in the Appendix. A study of these charts shows that the movement of the stock market tends to be cyclical. Using a combination of techniques to follow the price fluctuations, the twenty year time period since 1964 has been divided into market trading cycles that are defined as follows.

A trading cycle begins at the last intermediate NYSE Index high. The decline which follows must reach a downward momentum of sufficient magnitude to cause the market to become excessively oversold. The decline may continue for some time, perhaps for many months, but ultimately the market reaches a final low point. From here, the market begins to advance, taking it out of the oversold area, through the neutral area and finally into the overbought area. This is the crucial point in the cycle, for if the upmove is just a rally in a bear market, it will quickly fall back to the neutral zone, thus completing the cycle. However, if a new bull market develops, the index may remain in the overbought zone for as long as a year, while considerable profits are accumulated by investors. Eventually, however, the market reaches its final high point and then declines to the neutral zone once again, thus completing the trading cycle.

From 1964 to 1984 there were 27 market trading cycles as defined by this system. If one could have used the NYSE Index as a trading vehicle (that is, buying and selling the index as each signal developed) the results would have been as follows:

> Five trading cycles would be classed as bull markets, with profits ranging from 14.1% to 50.6%.

> One cycle, the terrible bear market of 1974, produced an acceptable loss of − 5.7%.

> The remaining 21 cycles would be called minor rallies with small gains or losses ranging from + 9.1% to − 3.1%.

The total gain for the 19½ year period was 395%. This compares to a "buy and hold" strategy which would have yielded 124% in profits while being invested 100% of the time. Our trading system was over three times more profitable than simply buying and holding. The results are really even better, since the interest earned while our capital was being held in money market funds was not included in the 395%.

Appendix A gives the specific data on the 27 market trading cycles and shows where they are located on charts of the NYSE Index. Appendix B lists every trading signal that was developed by the system over the 19½ year period. Appendix C gives the results that would have been obtained, assuming that the NYSE

Index itself was the trading vehicle. The final basic trading program was developed after careful computer analysis of the trading cycles. The results of the study were used to develop the automatic buy and sell rules that will be presented later.

MARKET TRADING SYSTEMS

Many market trading systems use a price index of some type to give buy and sell signals when the index crosses its moving average, either to the upside or the downside. Once the moving average is crossed to the upside, a single purchase of mutual fund shares (or common stocks) is made and held until a sell signal is given. This happens when the index recrosses the moving average to the downside. As long as the index remains above its moving average, the market is in an uptrend and profits are being accumulated. Moving averages may be of any length, from a few days to as long as 52 weeks. The price index may be a market index, like the Dow Jones Industrial Index or the NYSE Index, or it may be calculated from the prices of a group of mutual funds. This gives what is usually called a composite index.

The problem with any moving average trading system is that, as the length of the moving average time period is shortened, the number of whipsaws (false buy and sell signals) increases, trading frequency increases, and the number of unprofitable trades increases. On the other hand, as the moving average time period is lengthened, the buy signals come later and a larger portion of the market upmove is missed, often to the point of buying right at the top of the market. These moving average systems are defensive—they keep you out of all bear markets. However, they tend to produce many small losses while waiting for the eventual bull market to arrive. Hopefully, the losses will be recovered, along with satisfactory gains during the bull market. Unfortunately, significant bull markets come along only every few years. During my study of the NYSE Index over the 20 year period, many different moving average trading systems were tested, but none were found to be even half as profitable as the trading system developed here.

Other trading systems use a set of technical indicators to determine the state of the economy, or the stock market, or both. When a majority of indicators are favorable, a buy signal is given. Equities are held until the indicators turn unfavorable and a sell signal is given. Many technicians study chart patterns to determine when an individual stock should be purchased or sold.

Most investors do not have either the time or the experience to use their own systems. Therefore, they often subscribe to an advisory service that will give the buy and sell signals and tell them what stocks or funds to buy. Finding an advisory service that is suitable for your own investment objectives is probably as difficult as finding good stocks. Even the best and most expensive services are often dead wrong in picking market turns. Performance leadership among these advisory services rotates continuously.

HOW THE TRADING SYSTEM WORKS

The trading system which we will now develop is based upon an analysis of market cycles for timing the purchase and sale of no-load mutual funds that are used for trading. We will attempt to make our initial purchase of shares as we approach a market cycle bottom. It is our intention to accumulate a large inventory of fund shares by means of a unique system of downward cost averaging. This means that as the market decline continues, we will purchase more and more shares at lower prices. We will then hold our shares until the market makes its move toward the upper portion of the cycle. If a bull market develops, we will be in an excellent position to reap maximum financial rewards. If the move turns out to be just a rally in a bear market, we will sell out with a small gain, or perhaps even a small loss. If we are dead wrong and the market turns against us by continuing to decline far beyond the normal, we use a safety sell mechanism to bail us out and reduce our loss. The really big profits are made in the bull markets that come along every few years, and account for about 90% of all gains.

On occasion, a major market upmove will commence before we are fully invested at the previous market bottom. In this case, we will take advantage of a moving average crossing to commit the remainder of our capital, so that we won't miss a major bull move.

After the market makes a significant advance and moves into the overbought area of the cycle, an automatic sell plan is put into effect. The type of sell plan used will depend upon whether we have identified the upmove as a bull market or merely a short market rally. In any event, we will attempt to sell, not at the very top of the cycle, but after we are convinced that the upmove is over and the market has fallen back into the neutral zone.

FOLLOWING THE MARKET TRADING CYCLE

In order to define a market trading cycle and identify exactly where we are in that cycle, we will start by recording the NYSE Index on a daily basis, and use the index to calculate the 50-day exponential moving average (EA) of the index. Then we will use this EA to calculate an oscillator, which tells us whether the market is in the overbought or oversold area and to what degree. The oscillator is the heart of the trading system. Its movement generates the initial buy signal, follows the transition from the buying phase to the selling phase, and finally flashes the all important sell signal. On a weekly basis, we will use the Friday close of the NYSE Index to calculate its 39-week exponential moving average. In the event that we are not fully invested, the upside crossing of the 39-week EA by the NYSE Index triggers the final buy signal in the cycle and has us fully invested.

These simple calculations are all that are required to fully implement the basic system for trading. For the extra busy, the calculations take but a minute or two to complete. Later, some additional strategies will be presented to "fine tune" the system and improve the profit potential, while also reducing the risk involved.

THE OSCILLATOR

The use of an oscillator to determine if the market is overbought or oversold was described by Appel and Hitschler* as well as by others. In this system, the oscillator is, by definition, the percent difference between the NYSE Index and its 50-day exponential moving average. The oscillator is actually a measure of market momentum. If the NYSE Index rises significantly above its average value for the past 50 days, the market is said to be overbought, with the connotation that it should eventually fall back toward its average value. Similarly, if the index declines severely and the oscillator takes on a large negative value, the market is said to be oversold and the expectation is that it will move back up toward its average value. Therefore, the oscillator is simply a measure of the divergence between the NYSE Index and its average value over the last 50 days. It should be noted that, no matter how much the market is overbought or oversold, there is no practical way to determine in advance how long it will remain that way or when it will return to the neutral zone.

The NYSE Index oscillator was calculated on a daily basis beginning with the publication of the index in 1964. As long as the market is relatively stable, the index diverges only one or two percent from its 50-day EA. A good example of market stability was the period between April, 1976 and April, 1978, when the oscillator remained between +3.8 and −4.6 for over two years. The NYSE Index itself fluctuated only between 48 and 58 during that entire time. Traders do not make much money in stable

---

* Appel, G. and Hitschler, W.F., "Stock Market Trading Systems," Chapter 10, 1980; Dow Jones-Irwin, Homewood, Illinois

markets, so it can be seen that this was not a good time period to trade.

Occasionally, the market will undergo a strong advance or decline and the oscillator will respond by moving into the 5 to 10 range. This is the area of the excessively overbought or oversold market. On rare occasions, the market advance or decline will be so powerful that the oscillator will exceed 10 (plus or minus). For example, during the devastating bear market of 1974, the oscillator actually reached a value of − 14.6, the lowest ever recorded. It's still hard to believe, but between October, 1973 and October, 1974 the market gave up almost one-half of its total value. On the other hand, during the great bull market of 1982-1983, the oscillator reached a high value of + 12.7. Between August 1982 and July 1983, the market gained over 67% in value, as measured by the change in the NYSE Index.

A study of the oscillator charts reveals that most bull markets are preceded by sharp and extended declines near the end of the previous bear market, creating an excessively oversold area. This type of sell-off may have happened several times during the previous bear market, leading to rallies which appear to be the beginning of a new bull market. They then prove to be false starts. When this happens, that is, when the market becomes excessively oversold, it is our intention to become fully invested, just in case the next rally turns out to be the real thing. There is no way to predict in advance if the next upward move will be the beginning of a new bull market or just another rally in a bear market. Therefore, we will become invested and wait out the many false starts in order to be prepared for the real ones.

We will also use the oscillator to identify whether the current market climate is bullish or bearish. This will influence somewhat our next entry into the market cycle. For example, if in a previous cycle the oscillator fell to a value below − 8.0, we will take this as a major bear market signal. In this case, as we move into the next cycle, we will wait until the oscillator declines to a value of − 5.0 before buying any shares to begin our accumulation plan. However, if the oscillator reached a value of + 6.0 in a previous cycle, it signals that the market climate is bullish and we will be ready to reenter the market somewhat sooner at the start of the next cycle. In this case a decline in the oscillator to only − 3.0 will trigger the first buy signal to start our share accumulation plan.

This adjustment to bull and bear signals is recommended because after a bear market signal (osc. = − 8.0), we expect the bear market to continue and therefore we want to use more caution. After a bull market signal (osc. = + 6.0) we want to enter the next cycle somewhat earlier, as the market may not accommodate us by declining to an oscillator value of − 5.0.

A share accumulation plan was devised to compromise for the inability to accurately define a market bottom. With this plan, more and more shares are purchased at lower prices as the market decline continues. The market cycle charts show that only rarely did the market remain in the excessively oversold area for more than a few months after the first buy signal was given. With the share accumulation plan, we are almost always able to sell for a profit, even after the most modest market rally. It is of vital importance to participate fully in any new bull market.

Continuing our study of the oscillator charts, we note that there is a point during a market rally that signals the end of the buying phase and the beginning of the selling phase. Finally, we note that if we are participating in a bull market, we have to be very careful not to sell too soon.

It was by exhaustive analysis of all of the oscillator chart data that numerical values were eventually assigned to the oscillator, so that it could be used to automatically trigger the buy and sell signals which define this trading system. It was also necessary to devise a money management plan which would achieve optimum profits. This was done by computer analysis of the twenty-seven market trading cycles. Having completed this work, it was now possible to write a set of buy and sell rules which would govern all mutual fund trading. Having a set of rules to follow makes the system automatic and removes human emotion and judgement from trading which, I have found through experience, leads to generally poor results.

BUY AND SELL RULES

Bull Market Buy Rules

1. Buy shares in a selected no-load mutual fund with $1,000 when the NYSE Index oscillator falls to − 3.0. The NYSE Index value on this date will be the *first buy signal point.*

2. Buy additional fund shares with 40% of your starting capital when the NYSE Index declines another 3.5% from the *first buy signal point.*

3. Buy additional shares with 40% of your starting capital when the NYSE Index declines another 3.5% from the *second buy signal point.*

4. Buy additional shares with all your remaining capital when the NYSE Index declines another 3.5% from the *third buy signal point.* The accumulation of fund shares in a declining market is now complete.

Bear Market Buy Rules

1. Buy shares in a selected no-load mutual fund with $1,000 when the NYSE Index oscillator falls to − 5.0. The NYSE Index value on this date will be the *first buy signal point.*

2. Buy additional shares of the fund with 40% of your starting capital when the NYSE Index declines another 3% from the *first buy signal point.*

3. Buy additional shares with 40% of your starting capital when the NYSE Index declines another 3% from the *second buy signal point.*

4. Buy additional shares with all your remaining capital when the NYSE Index declines another 3% from the *third buy signal point.* The accumulation of fund shares in a declining market is now complete.

Moving Average Buy Signal

If, after making one or more purchases of shares, the market advances so that the NYSE Index crosses its 39-week exponential moving average to the upside and the oscillator has advanced to +2.0, purchase shares of the fund with all of your remaining capital.

Sell Rules

1. When the oscillator rises to +2.0 after one or more fund purchases have been made, the sell plan is put into effect. Sell all shares if the oscillator now declines to 0.

2. If the oscillator rises to +6.0 or higher, a new bull market is signalled. In this case, a different sell plan is used. When the oscillator first declines to 0, do not sell, but calculate a stop-loss sell point which is 2% below the current NAV of the mutual fund. If the market continues to decline, sell all shares when the stop-loss sell point is penetrated. If, however, the market rallies and the oscillator rises back to +2.0, sell all shares when the oscillator next falls back to 0.

Safety Signals

1. The safety sell signal is flashed when the NYSE Index declines 3% below the fourth buy signal point, regardless of which buy plan was used. Sell all shares except for $1,000 worth when this point is reached.

2. Start the cycle over again if the NYSE Index declines another 3% below the safety sell signal point, or if the oscillator advances to 0 and then declines to −5.0 again. This will now be the first buy point, but no purchase is necessary since we are already holding shares. If the next signal received is a moving average buy signal, buy shares with all remaining capital.

DISCUSSION OF THE BUY AND SELL RULES

The bull market and bear market buy rules are very similar, differing only in the value of the oscillator required for the first buy point and also in the magnitude of the market decline required for subsequent purchases. With this in mind, we will examine the rules one by one.

Buy Rule 1.

When the oscillator declines to a value of -3.0 (or -5.0 in a bear market), it signals that the market is seriously oversold and that it is time to begin the accumulation of no-load fund shares. Since we fully expect the market to go even lower and give us better buying opportunities, we will take only a pilot position at this time by opening an account with just $1,000.

This rule will absolutely prevent us from ever entering the market near the high point in a cycle, since it will have declined considerably from the last high before the oscillator can approach a value of -3.0 or -5.0.

Buy Rule 2.

When the market declines an additional 3.5% (3% in a bear market) from the first buy point as measured by the NYSE Index, it is time to make a substantial purchase of shares. We will now use 40% of our starting capital to buy shares, leaving about 50% of our capital remaining. Why 40% now? A tally of the buy signals during all twenty-seven market cycles since 1964 showed a high probability of getting either 2 or 3 buy signals due to a declining market in any trading cycle. Therefore, we will make substantial purchases on the second and third buy signals. The reason for the 3.5% decline in a bull market versus a 3% decline in a bear market is to compensate for the earlier entry in a bull market and to make the overall decline in both types of market about equal.

Buy Rule 3.

When this buy point is reached, the market will typically be down some 15%-20% from its last intermediate high point. We may not get a better opportunity to buy. Therefore, we will commit another 40% of our capital to purchase additional fund shares at a very attractive price. We will now be about 80% to 90% invested, holding the remaining portion of our capital for one final buying opportunity.

Buy Rule 4.

Occasionally, the market continues to decline to the point where a final purchase will be made at the lowest price in the cycle. However, it is far more likely that this remaining portion of our capital will be committed only after the market reverses and moves higher and the NYSE Index crosses its 39-week moving average to the upside.

Moving Average Buy Signal.

The action of the stock market will not always accommodate a neat downward averaging accumulation plan. Occasionally, it will decline only to the first buy point, then reverse to the upside, especially after a bull market signal. In this case we have no choice but to follow the trend and buy in when the index crosses its 39-week moving average. This undoubtedly will be the last buying opportunity in the cycle. We will now commit all of our remaining capital, just in case a new bull market has started without giving us a better bottom buying opportunity. The rally may be brief, but if we do not act here, we will miss out on any significant advance. It is better to take a small loss on this move than to miss out completely. In order to insure that we have a clear sell plan after the moving average signal, we will also wait until the oscillator has advanced to +2.0 before buying and then we will immediately put the sell plan into effect.

Sell Rule 1.

After the share accumulation phase has been completed, we will normally hold our shares until the next rally begins. If this advance carries the oscillator well to the upside, as signalled by a move above +2.0, we will have substantial paper profits. These gains must be protected, in the event that the market turns to the downside. Therefore, the oscillator value of +2.0 will signal the transition from the buying phase to the sell plan. Any remaining capital will be invested on the upward crossing of the 39-week moving average. As long as the oscillator remains in plus territory, the market advance is intact and we will hold on to our shares. However, if the oscillator falls to 0, penetrating the 50-day moving average to the downside, we will sell all of our shares and realize a profit. Penetration of the 50-day moving average could be temporary and the market might rally. On the other hand, any time the NYSE Index is below its 50-day moving average (oscillator less than 0), the market is in a downtrend and we could soon see our profits evaporate. Better to take the profits.

Sell Rule 2.

This rule is used to guide us when we hit the trading jackpot; fully invested in a new bull market. During the initial weeks and even months of a bull market, the momentum of the advance will carry the oscillator to extreme high values as institutions and traders rush to buy equities. The possibility of a new long term bull market is signalled by a move of the oscillator above +6.0. We must now be very careful not to sell too soon in any possible bull market. Therefore, if a market decline carries the oscillator below zero, we will not sell immediately, but will calculate a selling point that is 2% below the current asset value of each fund that we hold. Then, if the fund NAV falls below that point, we will liquidate our positions. In practically every case, the market will rally from here and go on to new highs. The rally will be defined by an advance of the oscillator to above +2.0. Now when the oscillator next falls to zero, we will sell all shares, since this second appearance of weakness often signals the end of the bull market.

Safety Rule 1.

This rule is needed for preservation of capital in the event we encounter a severe bear market, such as the 1970 or 1974 bear markets. After we have made all four purchases in a declining market, we will calculate a stop sell point that is 3% below the last (fourth) buy point. If the NYSE Index continues to decline and it closes below this point, we will immediately liquidate nearly all of our shares, holding on to approximately $1,000 worth in order to keep our account open in the event that the Safety Buy Rule 2 is triggered.

Safety Rule 2

If we have sold nearly all of our shares according to Safety Rule 1 above, we are even more anxious to participate in the forthcoming market advance, since it is likely to be a good one. Therefore, if the NYSE Index declines another 3% from the above sell point, we will now take this as the first buy signal and start the market cycle over. This safety sell routine is an unlikely event and has not occurred even once in the last ten years. However, we must have a safety rule available to insure the preservation of our capital. If this safety sell rule comes into effect, one should become aware of the tax code rules concerning "wash sales."

To further clarify the use of the safety sell rule, let's examine the 1970 market cycle. We were using the bear market buy rules and the first buy signal came on January 28, when the oscillator declined below −5.0. Buy points for the NYSE Index were calculated as follows:

Buy 1	48.59
Buy 2	47.13
Buy 3	45.72
Buy 4	44.35
Sell	43.02
Buy 1	41.73

After four purchases had been made, the market continued to decline and closed at 42.17 on May 12. At this sell point, all shares were liquidated except for $1,000 worth. Two days later, the Buy 1 point was reached. No action was required, since we were already holding our account open. The market continued downward and we soon became fully invested for the second time in this cycle with a NYSE Index average price of 38.96. A new bull market now began and our shares were finally sold on May 18, 1971 at 55.52. The safety sell signal took us out of the market with a loss of 7.5%. However, we realized a gain of 42.5% after the repurchase of shares, giving us an overall gain of 31.8% for the entire trading cycle.

There is the rare possibility that after a safety sell signal has been given, the market could reverse to the upside and begin a strong advance without having given us an opportunity to buy in at lower and lower prices. In this event, we will use the moving average buy signal to become fully invested.

RISK

Trading the market with this system is not without risk. In the prior discussion of market trading cycles, it was pointed out that during the 27 cycles since 1964, a significant loss was realized in only one of these cycles—the bear market of 1974. That loss amounted to just 5.7%, but no doubt it would have been worse if we actually had been trading aggressive no-load mutual funds at that time. The volatility of aggressive funds makes them gain or lose about twice as fast as the NYSE Index. For example, had an investor been trading the Stein Roe Capital Opportunities Fund during that bear market, the loss would have been 9.2%, certainly a tolerable loss in that severe bear market.

Consider those investors using the standard "buy and hold" approach. During that bear market, they stood by helplessly and watched their portfolios diminish to less than half their value. It would be many years before they recovered those losses.

The justification for accepting high risk is high reward. According to Lipper Analytical Services, Inc., the best performing mutual fund for the five year period ending December 31, 1984 was the Fidelity Magellan Fund with a gain of 314%. Using the basic system and including the interest earned at the short term Treasury Bill rate for the time periods when no fund shares were owned, trading the Constellation Growth Fund would have yielded a gain of 444% over a similar time period (from the October 19, 1979 buy signal to the November 16, 1984 sell signal).

The ten top performing mutual funds and their percentage gains over the five year period ending December 31, 1984 were:

Rank	Fund	5 Year Gain
1	**Magellan Fund**	314%
2	**Lindner Dividend**	247%
3	**Lindner Fund**	220%
4	**Vanguard Qual. Div. 1**	214%
5	**Phoenix Stock**	213%
6	**Phoenix Growth**	201%
7	**American Capital Pace**	201%
8	**United Vanguard Fund**	190%
9	**NEL Growth Fund**	185%
10	**Loomis-Sayles Capital**	183%

The average gain of the top ten best performing mutual funds was 217%, about one-half the gain of the Constellation Growth Fund using the basic trading system. It is also interesting to note that the Constellation Fund itself was up just 75% in the same five year time period. The basic trading system had the effect of increasing the return of the fund by almost 6 times while subjecting capital to risk only about two-thirds of the time.

After these considerations, it would seem that the risk is relatively low; much less than for a constant investment in one mutual fund using a buy and hold approach. The rewards have certainly been vastly improved. Therefore, it can be concluded that the risk/reward ratio is extremely favorable for the trading system.

THE TRADING SYSTEM IN ACTION

Before going into the detailed methods of calculations, let's examine the system using the buy and sell signals as they developed in both a bull market and a bear market. We'll look at the bull market of 1980 and the Autumn rally during the 1981 bear market. In this example, we will trade the Stein Roe Capital Opportunities Fund, an aggressive growth fund that invests mostly in companies that are listed in the Over-The-Counter market. Let us assume that we are new investors entering the market, and therefore had no previous bull or bear market signal to guide us. In this case we would use the bull market buy rules for our first cycle, as we do not want to miss out on a buying opportunity.

THE 1980 BULL MARKET

The NYSE Index declined steadily starting in February, 1980. This continued through March, until the oscillator fell to a value of −3.75 on March 6, thereby flashing a buy signal according to Buy Rule 1. By this time we would already have placed $10,000 of capital in the Stein Roe Cash Reserves (money market) Fund. A telephone call was made the next day, requesting that $1,000 be transferred to the Capital Opportunities Fund. Purchases and sales are always made on the day following the signal—the trade date.

On the day of the buy signal, the NYSE Index closed at 61.94. The remaining buy signal index values, as well as the safety sell point, were now calculated according to the plan. Each index value is 3.5% below the previous value:

Buy Number	NYSE Index
1	61.94
2	59.77
3	57.68
4	55.66
Sell	53.99

The net asset value (NAV) of the Capital Opportunities Fund on March 7, the day of the first purchase, was 15.68. Therefore, the $1,000 was used to purchase 63.8 shares, which were placed in our account.

On March 17, the NYSE Index fell to 58.22, which was well below the second buy point value of 59.77. On March 18, according to Buy Rule 2, our telephone call requested the transfer of $4,000 (40% of original capital) from the money market fund to the Capital Opportunities Fund. The NAV of the fund on that day was 14.67, so 272.7 more shares were added to our account. The market decline continued and one week later the NYSE Index closed at 56.47, triggering the third buy signal. Another $4,000 was exchanged for 293.3 shares of the fund. The final buy signal came on March 27, when the index fell to 55.30. Our remaining $1,000 was used to purchase 73.7 additional shares. We were now fully invested and had accumulated a total of 703.5 shares of the fund.

An interesting feature of this trading system can now be examined. Due to the continued decline in the NAV of the fund and the accumulation of shares at lower and lower prices, the average price paid for each share was 14.21. At the last purchase price of 13.56, our shares were worth $9,539 so that we now had a paper loss of $461. But that's the way the system is designed to work. We also were prepared to sell out if the safety sell point at 53.99 were penetrated, taking our loss but preserving our capital.

As it turned out, the market low for this trading cycle was reached on March 27 with the NYSE Index at 55.30. The market became steadier in April and managed to hold above the March low point. In May a strong advance got under way, and on May 19, the oscillator reached a value of +2.12 and the NYSE Index was well above its 39-week moving average. The move above +2.0 automatically put the sell plan into effect. Sell Rule 1 states that if the oscillator now were to fall back to 0, we would sell all shares. This was not the case, and on June 10 the oscillator advanced to +6.0, signalling the probability of a new bull market. Sell Rule 2 was now put into effect and we would be careful not to sell too soon.

Bull markets are wonderful events for the fully invested. The advance continued all through the summer and we were content to watch our profits grow. All good things must end, and late in September the oscillator finally fell to −0.3. Our immediate reaction was to calculate a stop-loss sell point for the fund to protect our profits in case the bull market had ended. On September 29, the day that the oscillator fell below 0, the fund NAV was 21.19. It was tempting to sell at this point, since we now had a profit of over 49%. Instead, we kept to the plan. The stop-loss point was calculated to be 20.77, 2% below the NAV of the fund on the day the oscillator declined to 0. We would sell if the NAV of the fund fell below that point. The market rallied during the first half of October, taking the oscillator back above +2.0. However, on October 30, the oscillator again fell below 0, and that gave us the final sell signal. The shares were sold on October 31 with the NAV of the fund at 23.43. The sale yielded a price of $16,483, for a gratifying profit of almost 65%. Our capital was returned to the money market fund to earn interest until the next buy signal.

The foregoing example describes a typical trading performance during a bull market. All trading cycles are not rewarded in that manner. Let us now examine the performance of the trading system in another cycle; the autumn rally in the 1981 bear market. Since the oscillator had reached a value of +6 in June, 1980, the bull market buy rules were still in effect. The three short cycles since then failed to produce any new major signal.

On August 24, 1981, the oscillator fell to a value of −3.94 and our account in the Capital Opportunities Fund was reopened with an exchange of $1,000 from the money market fund. With the accumulated interest, our capital had by now grown to about $18,000. The NAV of the fund was 20.54, so our initial purchase gave us 48.7 shares for our account. The market continued to decline during September, triggering subsequent buy signals so that we became fully invested and accumulated shares of the fund as follows:

Signal	Date	Fund NAV	Shares Purchased
1	8/25/81	20.54	48.7
2	9/ 4/81	19.26	373.8
3	9/18/81	18.57	387.7
4	9/28/81	18.11	143.6
		Total	953.8

A market rally during November brought the oscillator up to + 2.69 on November 2, putting the sell plan into effect. The advance ended there and no bull signal was received. The oscillator then declined to − 0.85 on November 16, triggering the sell signal. On November 17, with the NAV of the fund at 20.20, the shares were sold for $19,267. This amount was transferred back to the money market fund. The trading cycle yielded a profit of $1,267 or about 7%. During the September market decline, the oscillator fell below − 8, giving a major bear market signal. This meant that in the next market cycle, the oscillator must fall below − 5.0 to trigger the first buy signal.

Even though a return of 7% in only three months is a very reasonable profit, it should be emphasized again that the goal of the system is to become fully invested near the beginning of any new bull market. Since these markets cannot be identified until after the fact, this system will usually insure that we are invested when the bull market finally does materialize.

CALCULATIONS

In the previous discussions, reference was made to the use of moving averages of various lengths. It was also pointed out that the oscillator was the heart of the system. We will now show how these items are calculated and used to make the system work.

Moving Averages

A simple moving average is, by definition, an arithmetic average of a series of data points that moves through time. The primary purpose of a moving average is to smooth out the data, removing day-to-day fluctuations, so that the underlying trend in the data can be discovered. A 50-day *arithmetic* average of the NYSE Index would be calculated by adding together the values of the index for the last 50 days and then dividing the total by 50. To make this a 50-day *moving* average, tomorrow we would add the new value to the total and subtract the value that was obtained on the first day, or 51 days ago. Dividing the new total by 50 would again give us the average for the last 50 days. As we keep repeating this procedure day after day, it can be seen how the average moves through time.

Any time period may be selected for a moving average, depending on the intended use. It is not unusual to see moving average time periods as short as a few days and as long as a year. The moving average may be applied to data collected on a daily, weekly or even monthly basis.

A moving average allows us to determine the underlying trend in a set of data points. When applied to the NYSE Index, if the moving average is rising, the market is said to be in an uptrend. Conversely, if the moving average is falling, the market is in a downtrend. Many trading systems are based on moving averages. Signals for buying and selling may be flashed when the moving average is rising or falling, when the moving average is crossed by an index, or even when one moving average crosses another one.

A slightly modified version of a moving average, and the one used exclusively with this trading system, is the *exponential* moving average. This moving average has two advantages over the arithmetic average: it is weighted somewhat so that the most recent data carries more weight than the oldest data; it is also much simpler to calculate while producing similar results. The weight assignment to the more recent data is accomplished by using a "smoothing constant." To calculate a smoothing constant that gives a result that is almost equivalent to an arithmetic moving average, use the following equation:

$$\text{Constant} = \frac{2}{(N + 1)}$$

where N is the number of data points or days in the moving average. The smoothing constant for a 50-day exponential average would be:

$$\text{Constant} = \frac{2}{(50 + 1)} = 0.0392 = 0.04$$

The 50-day exponential moving average is calculated by multiplying the latest NYSE Index by .04, the smoothing constant, and adding the result to the product obtained by multiplying the previous exponential average by (1 − .04), or .96:

$$\text{Exp. Avg.} = (\text{NYSE Index} \times .04) + (\text{EA} \times .96)$$

where,

Exp. Avg.   = new or today's exponential average
EA   = last or yesterday's exponential average

For the very first calculation use yesterday's index in place of yesterday's EA. Let us assume that the most recent value for the 50-day EA of the NYSE Index was 41.372. The new closing value for the Index was 42.92. The new exponential average would be calculated as follows:

$$\begin{aligned}
\text{Exp. Avg.} &= (42.92 \times .04) + (41.372 \times .96) \\
&= 1.717 + 39.717 \\
&= 41.434
\end{aligned}$$

The exponential average must be calculated for 50 consecutive days before it is completely valid. It is not difficult to obtain the last 50 values for the index in the local library from back issues of the Wall Street Journal or most any daily newspaper. We will sometimes refer to the 50-day exponential moving average as the .04 EA.

THE OSCILLATOR

Having now obtained a valid 50-day moving average of the NYSE Index, it is a simple matter to calculate the oscillator. By definition, the oscillator is the percent difference between the NYSE Index and its .04 EA. Using the above values for these items, the oscillator is calculated as follows:

$$\text{Osc.} = \frac{(\text{NYSE Index} - .04\,\text{EA}) \times 100}{.04\,\text{EA}}$$

$$= \frac{(42.92 - 41.434) \times 100}{41.434}$$

$$= \frac{1.486 \times 100}{41.434}$$

$$= 3.59$$

It may have been noted in this example that the 50-day exponential moving average is increasing. Therefore, the trend of the market is up. The oscillator shows that the current value of the NYSE Index is 3.59% above the moving average. All of the above calculations can be done in a few seconds on even the most inexpensive hand calculators.

While the above calculations are all that are needed on a daily basis to put the trading system into effect, there is still one more calculation, to be done on a weekly basis, to complete the data needed for the system. This is the 39-week exponential moving average. In this case, we will need the weekly closing values for the NYSE Index for the previous 39 weeks (9 months). This data may also be obtained at the library from back issues of any newspaper.

The smoothing constant for a 39-week exponential moving average would be calculated as follows:

$$\text{Constant} = 2/(N+1) = 2/40 = 0.05$$

The 39-week EA is calculated in exactly the same way as the 50-day EA:

$$\text{Exp. Avg.} = (\text{Friday's NYSE Index} \times .05) + (\text{EA} \times .95)$$

If last Friday's EA were 43.222 and the index closed this Friday at 44.87, the new EA would be calculated as follows:

$$
\begin{aligned}
\text{EA} &= (44.87 \times .05) + (43.222 \times .95) \\
&= 2.243 + 41.061 \\
&= 43.304
\end{aligned}
$$

After a few practice trials it will be obvious that these are very simple calculations. Now that we have the methods of calculation available, let us put the system to work. In this example, we go back to 1978 and begin our worksheet as of October 13. As the buy signals develop, we will again use the NAV data for the Constellation Growth Fund to follow the purchase and sale of shares. Our worksheet will look like this:

Date	NYSE Index	.04 EA	Oscillator	Remarks	39-Week EA
10/13/78	58.93	58.039	+ 1.54		55.318
10/16/78	57.80	58.029	− 0.39		
10/17/78	56.89	57.983	− 1.89		
10/18/78	56.40	57.920	− 2.62		
10/19/78	55.71	57.831	− 3.67	Buy Signal	
10/20/78	54.76	57.708	− 5.11		55.290
10/23/78	54.79	57.592	− 4.86		
10/24/78	54.46	57.446	− 5.23		
10/25/78	54.34	57.341	− 5.23		
10/26/78	53.48	57.187	− 6.48		

Due to the sharp decline in the NYSE Index, the oscillator fell to −3.67 on October 20, triggering the first buy signal. This meant that the market was excessively oversold and had sufficient downward momentum to invite our buying into a pilot position. Now we will calculate the future buy point values for the NYSE Index. Each new buy point requires a 3.5% additional decline in the index. The oscillator gives only the first buy signal. It is the further action of the market index itself that determines subsequent buy points.

Next Buy Points

Buy 2	**53.76**
Buy 3	**51.88**
Buy 4	**50.06**

Since the first buy signal came from a Friday's market activity, the calculations were made on Saturday morning and a check for $1,000 was sent in the mail the same day. It is not necessary to rush this purchase by special mail, since we are only opening our account at this time and the size of the purchase is small. Once the account is opened, we will make subsequent purchases by telephone. We fully expect lower prices in the days ahead and are saving larger commitments of capital until then.

When we received our confirmation statement, we noted that the share purchase had been made on Tuesday, October 24 with the NAV of the fund at 7.36. Our $1,000, therefore, was used to purchase 135.9 shares of the fund. This is a good time to take care of another chore. Address a letter to the fund requesting redemption of your shares. Be sure to include the account number. Without dating the letter, take it to your bank and, in the presence of a bank officer, sign the letter exactly as your signature appeared on the application (along with any joint owner) and have the bank officer guarantee the signatures. This is a routine procedure for the bank and will probably be done without charge. Keep the letter until it is needed at the time of the next sell signal. Then it can be dated and mailed, using an overnight mail service.

Continuing with the data records, our worksheet would have been kept up to date as follows:

Date	Index	.04 EA	Oscillator	Remarks	39-Week EA
10/26/78	53.48	57.187	− 6.48	Second buy	
10/27/78	52.52	57.000	− 7.86		55.152
10/30/78	52.65	56.826	− 7.35		
10/31/78	51.67	56.620	− 8.74	Third buy	
11/ 1/78	53.79	56.507	− 4.81		
11/ 2/78	53.20	56.374	− 5.63		
11/ 3/78	53.49	56.259	− 4.92		55.069
11/ 6/78	53.03	56.130	− 5.52		
11/ 7/78	52.22	55.973	− 6.71		
11/ 8/78	52.49	55.834	− 5.99		
11/ 9/78	52.52	55.701	− 5.71		
11/10/78	52.72	55.582	− 5.15		54.951
11/13/78	51.83	55.432	− 6.50		
11/14/78	51.36	55.269	− 7.07		
11/15/78	51.52	55.119	− 6.53		

The market continued to decline through the remainder of October, and when the NYSE Index fell to 53.48 on October 26 the second buy signal was triggered. It was now time to make a significant purchase of fund shares, according to Buy Rule 2. The next day a phone call was made to the fund and an order was placed to purchase shares at that day's closing price in the amount of $4,000. Our starting capital was assumed to be $10,000, and we were to use 40% of our starting capital for this second purchase. A check for $4,000 was put in the mail on the same day. The fund NAV at the close was 6.62, so we were able to buy 604.2 shares, which were added to our account. It should also be noted that on October 31 the oscillator fell to − 8.74, triggering a major bear market signal. This was of no immediate concern, but it would affect the buy rules for the next market cycle unless it were cancelled by a new bull market signal.

The trend of the market continued downward and the third buy signal was given on October 31, when the index fell below our buy point of 51.88. Again we called the fund to order shares in the amount of $4,000, as directed by Buy Rule 3. Again, the check followed by mail. The NAV of the fund was now 7.08, so 565.0 shares were purchased, bringing the total holdings to 1,305.1 shares. Our shares now had a market value of $9,423, a paper profit of $240. This was somewhat surprising, since normally we expect to make our purchases at lower and lower prices. Usually we will have a small paper loss as we average our purchase price downward.

As it turned out, the market low for this trading cycle was reached on November 14, with the NYSE Index at 51.36. Our fourth buy point, at 50.06, was not reached in the current downtrend. The market turned upward during December, and on January 3 the index closed at 54.57 (which was just higher than the 39-week moving average). However, before we have a moving average buy signal, the oscillator also has to be above +2.0. Therefore, we must wait. Just two days later, the oscillator jumped to +2.44 and the buy signal was completed. The remainder of our capital was now committed to the fund. These points may be examined on our worksheet, which looked like this:

Date	Index	.04 EA	Oscillator	Remarks	39-Week EA
12/22/78	53.77	53.980	− 0.40		54.569
12/26/78	54.36	53.995	+ 0.67		
12/27/78	53.90	53.991	− 0.18		
12/28/78	53.68	53.979	− 0.56		
12/29/78	53.62	53.965	− 0.65		54.521
1/ 2/79	53.93	53.963	− 0.07		
1/ 3/79	54.57	53.987	+ 1.07		
1/ 4/79	55.05	54.030	+ 1.88		
1/ 5/79	55.41	54.085	+ 2.44	MA Buy; Sell Plan Now In Effect	54.566

The underlying trend of the market had now turned up, as indicated by both the 50-day moving average (.04 EA) and the 39-week moving average. These were both moving up. We were now fully invested and holding a total of 1,435.5 shares of the Constellation Growth Fund, with the average price paid for each share calculated to be 6.97. The buying phase was now completed. You may have noted that the market value of our shares at the time of the last purchase was $11,010. We were already holding a paper profit of 10%. This is due to the power of the unique downward dollar cost averaging technique, which is an important aspect of this trading system.

THE SELL PLAN

The buying program is always completed when we become fully invested, but the sell plan does not go into effect until the oscillator rises to a value of +2.0. In this example, the sell plan went into effect on January 5, the same day as the moving average buy signal was given. Continuing with our worksheet:

Date	Index	.04 EA	Oscillator	Remarks	39-Week EA
1/19/79	55.85	54.620	+2.25		54.694
1/22/79	55.92	54.672	+2.28		
1'/23/79	56.27	54.736	+2.80		
1/24/79	56.07	54.789	+2.33		
1/25/79	56.62	54.862	+3.20		
1/26/79	56.99	54.947	+3.71		54.808
1/29/79	56.85	55.024	+3.32		

We will now continue to collect our data and keep observing the oscillator for the next signal. If it advances to +6.0, a new bull market will be signalled. If, however, the oscillator declines to 0 before reaching +6.0, we will sell all shares immediately, since the rally is over. In this example, no bull signal was forthcoming and the oscillator soon declined to 0, flashing the sell signal:

Date	Index	.04 EA	Oscillator	Remarks	39-Week EA
1/31/79	55.99	55.123	+1.57		
2/ 1/79	56.00	55.158	+1.52		
2/ 2/79	55.79	55.183	+1.10		54.858
2/ 5/79	55.01	55.176	−0.31	Sell signal	
2/ 6/79	54.99	55.169	−0.33		
2/ 7/79	54.47	55.141	−1.22		

The sell signal was flashed on February 5, when the NYSE Index fell to 55.01 and carried the oscillator to −0.31. Since the Constellation Growth Fund does not accept sell orders by telephone, we sent our redemption letter by the Post Office overnight delivery service. The redemption letter, with the signatures already guaranteed, had been written some time ago. This allowed us to avoid any further delay and to sell our shares on February 7, with the NAV at 7.42. The liquidation value of the shares was $10,651, giving us a profit of $651, or 6.5%. When the redemption check was received, the capital was placed in our regular money market fund to collect interest until the next trading cycle began.

SUMMARY

We have now completed the first trading cycle in our six year test program. We had to make two simple calculations each day and one more each week. All signals were developed automatically. We made no predictions on the future course of the market, and it was only necessary to act on the signals as directed by the buy and sell rules. As it turned out, this market cycle was only a brief rally in a relatively flat stock market. Our trading system had us fully invested for only a few months, and we exited the market with a modest profit. The bull market that we anticipated failed to materialize, so we had to retreat to the safety of our money market to await future developments. The bull market was still more than a year away.

TRADING SIGNALS

In the previous section, we studied the methods for calculating the required moving averages and the oscillator. We also examined the 1978 trading cycle in detail, reviewing the calculations on a daily basis and showing how each signal developed as a result of the movement of the stock market. The entire system was shown to be automatic—when the signals were flashed we simply followed the rules for buying or selling a no-load mutual fund. It was not necessary for us to make predictions on the future course of the market. It was also noted that the entire trading cycle was over in less than 3-1/2 months and that it would be another 8-1/2 months until the next buy signal. It can now be seen why the system requires both patience and discipline. We will often watch the market undergo a sharp rally and wonder why we are not participating. Of course, we will also watch the sharp declines and be glad that we are not participating.

There were eleven trading cycles during the six year test period between October, 1978 and November, 1984. We will now review the history of the test period by listing every signal that was encountered during that period and what action was taken. The complete list of trading signals is given in the following tables.

TRADING SIGNALS

A Summary of All Oscillator and NYSE Index Signals That Required Some Action While Trading a No-Load Mutual Fund Between October, 1978 and November, 1984

Date	Signal
10/19/78	Oscillator declines to -3.67, NYSE Index = 55.71. Purchase shares of a no-load mutual fund with $1,000. Next buy point = 53.76, a 3.5% decline in the NYSE Index.
10/26/78	NYSE Index = 53.48. Buy shares with 40% of capital. Next buy point = 51.88.

TRADING SIGNALS (Cont'd)

Date	Signal
10/31/78	NYSE Index = 51.67. Buy shares with 40% of capital. Next buy point = 50.06. Osc. = −8.74 − major bear signal.
1/ 5/79	NYSE Index = 55.41, 39-week EA = 54.56, oscillator = +2.44. This is a moving average buy signal. Buy shares with all remaining capital. Sell plan is in effect and now we are fully invested.
2/ 5/79	Osc. = −0.31. This is the sell signal. Sell all shares.
10/19/79	Osc. = −5.01, NYSE Index = 57.62. Purchase shares of the fund with $1,000. Next buy point = 55.89.
11/26/79	NYSE Index = 60.91, 39-week EA = 58.55, osc. = +2.86. Moving average buy signal. Purchase shares of the fund with all remaining capital. Sell plan in effect and now fully invested.
1/ 2/80	Osc. = −0.12 − sell signal. Sell all shares.
2/ 8/80	Osc. = +6.31 − major bull market signal.
3/ 6/80	Osc. = −3.75, NYSE Index = 61.94. Purchase shares of the fund with $1,000. Next buy point = 59.77.
3/17/80	NYSE Index = 58.22. Buy fund shares with 40% of capital. Next buy point = 57.36. Osc. = −8.08 − major bear market signal.
3/24/80	NYSE Index = 56.47. Buy fund shares with 40% of capital. Next buy point = 55.35.
3/27/80	NYSE Index = 55.30. Buy shares with all remaining capital. Now we are fully invested.
5/19/80	Osc. = +2.12, sell plan in effect.
6/10/80	Osc. = +6.00, bull market signal. Bull market sell plan in effect.

TRADING SIGNALS (Cont'd)

Date	Signal
9/29/80	Osc. = − 0.32, caution signal. Calculate stop-loss sell point that is 2% below the NAV of the fund. Sell if the fund closes below that point.
10/ 1/80	Osc. = + 2.47, market rally. Cancel Stop-loss point and sell all shares when the oscillator next declines to 0.
10/30/80	Osc. = − 1.10, sell signal. Sell all shares.
12/10/80	Osc. = − 3.46, NYSE Index = 73.78. Purchase shares of the fund with $1,000. Next buy point = 71.20.
12/22/80	NYSE Index = 77.94, 39-week EA = 71.04, Osc. = + 2.29. Moving average buy signal. Buy shares with all remaining capital. Sell plan in effect.
1/ 8/81	Osc. = − 0.78, sell signal. Sell all shares.
2/ 2/81	Osc. = − 4.45, NYSE Index = 72.67. Purchase shares of the fund with $1,000. Next buy point = 70.13.
3/13/81	NYSE Index = 77.19, 39-week EA = 72.98, Osc. = 2.94. Moving average buy signal. Purchase shares of the fund with all remaining capital. Sell plan in effect.
4/29/81	Osc. = − 0.05, sell signal. Sell all shares.
7/ 6/81	Osc. = − 3.28, NYSE Index = 73.99. Purchase shares of the fund with $1,000. Next buy point = 71.40.
8/11/81	NYSE Index = 77.65, 39-week EA = 75.28, Osc. = + 2.22. Moving average buy signal. Purchase shares of the fund with all remaining capital.
8/18/81	Osc. = − 0.72, sell signal. Sell all shares.
8/24/81	Osc. = − 3.94, NYSE Index = 72.92. Purchase shares with $1,000. Next buy point = 70.37.

TRADING SIGNALS (Cont'd)

Date	Signal
9/ 3/81	NYSE Index = 70.25, buy shares of the fund with 40% of capital. Next buy point = 67.90.
9/ 8/81	Osc. = − 8.09 − major bear market signal.
9/17/81	NYSE Index = 67.83. Buy shares of the fund with 40% of capital. Next buy point = 65.53.
9/25/81	NYSE Index = 64.96. Buy shares of the fund with all remaining capital. Now we are fully invested.
11/ 2/81	Osc. = + 2.69, sell plan in effect.
11/16/81	Osc. = − 0.85, sell signal. Sell all shares.
1/13/82	Osc. = − 5.60, NYSE Index = 66.63. Purchase shares of the fund with $1,000. Next buy point = 64.63.
2/22/82	NYSE Index = 64.55. Buy shares of the fund with 40% of capital. Next buy point = 62.69.
3/ 8/82	NYSE Index = 62.03. Buy shares of the fund with 40% of capital. Next buy point = 60.81.
4/ 8/82	Osc. = + 2.03, sell plan in effect.
5/18/82	Osc. = − 0.22, sell signal. Sell all shares.
6/17/82	Osc. = − 5.02, NYSE Index = 61.96. Purchase shares of the fund with $1,000. Next buy point = 60.10.
8/ 6/82	NYSE Index = 59.69. Buy shares of the fund with 40% of capital. Next buy point = 58.30.
8/20/82	Osc. = + 3.67, sell plan in effect.
8/23/82	NYSE Index = 66.36, 39-week EA = 65.65, osc. = + 6.09. Moving average buy signal and bull market signal. Buy shares with all remaining capital. Bull market sell plan in effect.
1/24/83	Osc. = − 0.17, caution signal. Calculate stop-loss sell point that is 2% below the NAV of the fund. Sell if the fund closes below that point.

TRADING SIGNALS (Cont'd)

Date	Signal
1/27/83	Osc. = +2.44, market rally. Cancel stop-loss point and sell all shares when the oscillator next declines to 0.
7/15/83	Osc. = −0.22, sell signal. Sell all shares.
8/ 8/83	Osc. = −3.34, NYSE Index = 92.19. Purchase shares of the fund with $1,000. Next buy point = 88.96.
9/ 6/83	NYSE = 96.84, 39-week EA = 89.91, Osc. = +2.08. Moving average buy signal. Purchase shares of the fund with all remaining capital.
10/19/83	Osc. = −0.52, sell signal. Sell all shares.
2/ 6/84	Osc. = −4.04, NYSE Index = 91.43. Purchase shares of the fund with $1,000. Next buy point = 88.10
5/23/84	NYSE Index = 88.09. Purchase shares of the fund with 40% of capital. Next buy point = 85.02.
8/ 2/84	NYSE Index = 90.77, 39-week EA = 90.29, osc. = +3.18. Moving average buy signal. Purchase shares of the fund with remaining capital. Sell plan in effect.
8/ 9/84	Osc. = +6.69, bull market signal. Bull market sell plan in effect.
10/ 3/84	Osc. = −0.39, caution signal. Calculate stop-loss sell point that is 2% below NAV of the fund. Sell if the fund closes below that point.
10/18/84	Osc. = +2.67, market rally. Cancel stop-loss sell point. Sell all shares when the oscillator next declines to 0.
11/16/84	Osc. = −0.77, sell signal. Sell all shares.

TRADING RESULTS

Having developed the foregoing trading signals by simply following the buy and sell rules presented earlier, we can now examine the results that would have been achieved if we had acted on each signal. We will assume that we started trading with initial capital of $10,000, and that we bought and sold only the Constellation Growth Fund. Each first purchase of $1,000 was made by regular first class mail and was completed three days after the signal was received. All subsequent purchases were made by telephone on the day after the signal. Sale of the shares was accomplished by writing a letter requesting redemption, having the signatures guaranteed and sending it off using an overnight delivery service. This procedure required just one additional day to complete the sale, as compared to telephone exchange sales.

The trading results are given in two ways. The first table shows the results with all dividends, capital gain distributions and trading profits reinvested, but does not include any interest earned while our capital was placed in a money market fund awaiting reinvestment. The second table gives the results in the same way as the first table, but does include the interest from the money market funds. Both methods are shown in order to stress the importance of the earned interest in the overall program. Since our capital was invested in fund shares only about two-thirds of the time and in money market funds the remaining one-third of the time, the interest earned becomes an important contribution to profits.

TRADING RESULTS
Constellation Growth Fund

Trade Cycle	Invest	Avg.Price Per Share	Sale NAV	Sale Proceeds	Gain	New Capital
1	$10,000	6.97	7.42	$10,651	$ 651	$10,651
2	10,651	11.28	12.76	12,048	1,397	12,048
3	12,048	12.27	20.25	19,889	7,841	19,889
4	19,889	22.12	21.32	19,170	− 719	19,170
5	19,170	19.73	20.57	19,982	812	19,982
6	19,982	20.16	19.58	19,408	− 574	19,408
7	19,408	15.24	16.69	21,251	1,843	21,251
8	18,000	11.81	12.61	19,220	1,220	22,472
9	22,472	10.55	25.46	54,243	31,771	54,243
10	54,243	24.39	21.71	48,275	− 5,968	48,275
11	48,275	15.47	16.26	50,733	2,458	50,733

Total Gain $40,733   Percent Gain   407.33%

Percent/year   67.89%   Compounded   31.08%

Time - 6 Years

TRADING RESULTS
Constellation Growth Fund and Money Market Interest

Trade Cycle	Invest	Average Price	Sell NAV	Sale Proceeds	Gain	Interest	New Capital
1	$10,000	6.97	7.42	$10,651	$ 651	$ 770	$11,421
2	11,421	11.30	12.76	12,900	1,479	289	13,189
3	13,189	12.25	20.25	21,806	8,617	336	22,142
4	22,142	22.13	21.32	21,335	− 807	204	21,539
5	21,539	19.74	20.57	22,446	907	625	23,071
6	23,071	20.17	19.58	22,401	− 670	56	22,457
7	22,457	15.22	16.69	24,619	2,162	429	25,048
8	21,000	11.79	12.61	22,452	1,452	256	26,757
9	26,757	10.54	25.46	64,614	37,857	340	64,954
10	64,954	24.39	21.71	57,805	− 7,149	1,520	59,325
11	59,325	15.48	16.26	62,326	3,001	0	62,326

Total Gain $52,326   Percent Gain   523.26%

Percent/year   87.21%   Compounded   35.66%

Time - 6 Years

FREE BOOK!

Just send in this card to receive, absolutely FREE:

- Information describing an exciting new commodity trading book.

- Stock and Commodity Booklist featuring hundreds of current and classical techniques for profitable investing.

- The book, "100 Rules on How to Trade Profitably" by George Seamans (regular price $5.00.) The 100 rules are geared primarily for the active intermediate term trader. Seamans has been selected one of the 4 greatest Wall St. minds of the 20th century. Truly a classic.

  Absolutely Free!

PLEASE PRINT LEGIBLY OR TYPE

NAME _____

ADDRESS _____

CITY _____ STATE _____ ZIP _____

BUSINESS REPLY MAIL

FIRST CLASS MAIL   PERMIT NO. 11   BRIGHTWATERS, NY

POSTAGE WILL BE PAID BY ADDRESSEE

WINDSOR BOOKS
PO BOX 280
BRIGHTWATERS NY   11718-9806

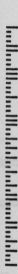

MARKET LEADERSHIP

Trading in the stock market seems to be dominated by two types of investors, institutional or otherwise—those who prefer the higher quality, more established companies listed on the New York Stock Exchange and those who prefer the smaller, faster growing companies in the Over-The-Counter market. Generally, there is good balance between the two markets—the price indices that represent them will advance or decline at about the same rate. Occasionally, however, there will be a significant imbalance in one or the other. During bear markets, it is not unusual for the OTC Index to decline faster than the NYSE Index, as investors seek more safety in the higher quality NYSE stocks. Conversely, during bull markets, many investors move to the stocks trading in the OTC market, so that index will advance faster than the NYSE Index. For example, during the 1982-1983 bull market, the advance was led by the OTC Index, which gained 106.7% at its peak on June 24, 1983. In that same time period, the NYSE Index gained 68.4%. Obviously, the OTC Index was leading the market upward.

The turn-around in market leadership came during August of 1983. Both markets began to decline toward the end of 1983. However, the decline in the OTC Index was far more severe than that in the NYSE Index. When the next rally began, it was the NYSE Index that led the way. This is not an unusual action for the market, especially after a long and powerful advance such as was experienced in 1982-1983. Savvy investors, having made large gains in volatile stocks in the OTC market, began taking profits by selling those stocks and reinvesting the proceeds in higher quality, blue chip stocks which trade on the New York Stock Exchange. Selling pressure was driving the OTC Index downward and buying pressure was pushing the NYSE Index up.

Had we as traders been alert to this action in the indices, we also would have switched our investments out of mutual funds that trade in OTC stocks and into funds that trade mostly in higher quality stocks on the New York Stock Exchange. Very aggressive funds, such as the Constellation Growth Fund and the Stein Roe Capital Opportunities Fund, that invest almost exclusively in stocks that trade in the OTC market would have been avoided. Instead, we would have switched our capital into higher quality funds, such as Selected American Shares Fund, Boston Capital Appreciation Fund or the Stein Roe Special Fund. In fact, each family of funds has a high quality equity mutual fund that serves as a basic fund intended for long term investors.

In order to determine which market is showing strong leaderhip, an index called "Market Momentum" was developed. It is defined as the annualized percent change in the 20-week exponential moving average of the indices, and is calculated on a weekly basis along with the 39-week moving average of the NYSE. Its calculation is not difficult. First, compute the 20-week EA of the two indices. Second, determine the percent change in each EA from the previous week. Third, multiply the results by 52 to annualize the data.

Let's examine the calculation of market momentum in more detail, using typical data in a time period somewhat before the bull market of 1982. At that time, and for a few weeks earlier, the values of the indices were as follows:

DATE	NYSE	OTC
6/ 4/82	63.42	174.82
6/11/82	63.94	173.55
6/18/82	61.74	168.50
6/25/82	62.72	170.48
7/ 2/82	61.99	170.05

The smoothing constant for a 20-week exponential average is 2 divided by 21, or .095. The equation for calculating the 20-week EA (.095 EA) for the NYSE Index is as follows:

$$EA = (NYSE \times .095) + (LWEA \times .905)$$

where,

$$\begin{aligned} \text{EA} &= \text{this week's .095 EA} \\ \text{LWEA} &= \text{last week's .095 EA} \end{aligned}$$

On June 4, 1982, the .095 EA was 66.725 and the .095 EA for the following week, June 11, would be calculated as follows:

$$\begin{aligned} \text{EA} &= (63.94 \times .095) + (66.725 \times .905) \\ &= (6.074 + 60.386) \\ &= 66.460 \end{aligned}$$

Market momentum, or the annualized percent change in the 20-week exponential moving average, can now be calculated for the week of June 11, as follows:

$$\text{MOM} = \frac{(\text{This week's EA} - \text{Last week's EA}) \times 100 \times 52}{\text{Last week's EA}}$$

$$= \frac{(66.460 - 66.725) \times 100 \times 52}{66.725}$$

$$= \frac{-0.265 \times 100 \times 52}{66.725}$$

$$= \frac{-1378.00}{66.725}$$

$$= -20.65$$

Having done all of the calculations for exponential averages and market momentum values for both the NYSE Index and the OTC Index, our weekly worksheet would look like this:

Part I—The Stock Market

Date	NYSE Index	.095 EA	NYSE MOM	OTC Index	.095 EA	OTC MOM
6/ 4/82	63.42	66.72	− 26.9	174.82	183.01	− 24.3
6/11/82	63.94	66.46	− 20.6	173.55	182.11	− 25.5
6/18/82	61.74	66.01	− 35.1	168.50	180.82	− 36.9
6/25/82	62.72	65.70	− 24.6	170.48	179.84	− 28.2
7/ 2/82	61.99	65.35	− 27.9	170.05	178.91	− 26.9

The values for market momentum have no meaning as absolute values, but are used exclusively in this application to compare the performance of the two markets. In the above example, the two markets show about equal strength. Both are in strong downtrends, as evidenced by the steady decline in the 20-week moving averages (.095 EA's).

To illustrate divergence between the two markets, let us examine momentum data from another time period—such as January and February of 1984:

Next Buy Points

Buy 2   53.76
Buy 3   51.88
Buy 4   50.06

Since the first buy signal came from Friday's market activity, the calculations were made on Saturday morning and a check for $1,000 was sent in the mail the same day. It is not necessary to rush this purchase by special mail, since we are only opening our account at this time and the size of the purchase is small. Once the account is opened, we will make subsequent purchases by telephone. We fully expect lower prices in the days ahead and are saving larger commitments of capital until then.

When we received our confirmation statement, we noted that the share purchase had been made on Tuesday, October 24 with the NAV of the fund at 7.36. Our $1,000, therefore, was used to purchase 135.9 shares of the fund. This is a good time to take care of another chore. Address a letter to the fund requesting redemption of your shares. Be sure to include the account number. Without dating the letter, take it to your bank and in the presence of a bank officer, sign the letter exactly as your signature appeared on the application (along with any joint owner) and have the bank officer guarantee the signature. This is a routine procedure for the bank and will probably be done without charge. Keep the letter until it is needed at the time of the next sell signal. Then it can be dated and mailed, using an overnight mail service.

Continuing with the data records, our worksheet would have been kept up to date as follows:

Date	NYSE Index	.095	NYSE MOM	OTC Index	.095 EA	OTC MOM
1/27/84	94.77	95.51	− 4.2	273.18	284.45	− 21.5
2/ 3/84	92.98	95.26	− 13.1	264.01	282.51	− 35.5
2/10/84	90.07	94.77	− 26.9	254.04	279.81	− 49.8
2/17/84	89.59	94.28	− 27.0	251.33	277.10	− 50.3
2/24/84	90.49	93.92	− 19.9	251.44	274.66	− 45.8

This data shows that, even though both indices are in strong downtrends, the NYSE Index was performing much, much better in relation to the OTC Index. These observations will have more meaning if we examine the momentum charts (in the Appendix) that cover the six year test period. We can see that the OTC Index momentum consistently outperformed the NYSE Index momentum, especially during bull markets. Near the end of the sharp declines in October of 1978 and 1979, the OTC momentum fell much faster and farther than did the NYSE momentum. However, when the next advance started, the OTC quickly recovered and assumed its leadership. During the 1981-1982 bear market, the momentums stayed close together, except at the bottoms of sharp declines. This pattern repeated itself without change until the end of the 1982-1983 bull market, when a serious deviation took place. The OTC Index lost its upward lead in August of 1983 and then continued to decline at a much faster pace than did the NYSE Index. This in itself was quite unusual. But the OTC Index did not come back and overtake the NYSE Index even once during the next eighteen months. It was not until January of 1985 that the "normal" relationship between the two market indices was restored. In the meantime, a great deal of damage was done to the OTC Index, having lost over 25% of its value while the NYSE Index was declining a mere 4.3%.

Observant investors who were monitoring both markets during this time period understood that the OTC Index was undergoing severe and obvious deterioration and was clearly signalling caution. The safe thing to do here was to avoid investing in the OTC market until it had regained its normal leadership position. This type of maneuvering is not at all difficult for investors who are alert to the situation. It is only a matter of buying into high quality no-load mutual funds.

Having completed this review of market momentum data, two courses of action come to mind to take advantage of market leadership. The first is to avoid all investments in mutual funds that hold nearly all of their assets in stocks of OTC companies during time periods when momentum data clearly shows that the OTC market has lost its leadership. A good example of this point was the market trading cycle that started with the buy signal of February 7, 1984. At that time we were prepared by the momentum data to make our investments in a New York Stock Exchange-oriented mutual fund, rather than an OTC-oriented fund. It would also be our intention to remain invested in this type of fund until the OTC market again regained its leadership. In retrospect, this did not happen during the entire trading cycle that ended with the November 16th sell signal. In fact, the OTC Index did not regain its leadership until January, 1985.

The second course of action is more subtle, and may not be too important. During the test period, it was noted that after the two long bull markets (1980 and 1982-83), the very next trading cycle favored NYSE-oriented mutual funds. Apparently, the end of a good bull market is a time for investors to rotate to higher quality. Therefore, on the buy signals of December 10th, 1980, and August 8th, 1983, no harm would be done, and a considerable amount of money would have been saved, by switching to a higher quality, NYSE-oriented fund. To sum up, after a bull market sell signal, switch to a quality fund for the next trading cycle.

Now that we have examined this aspect of changes in market leadership, let us look at the performance of some equity mutual funds during the 1984 trading cycle. If we assume that a total investment of $10,000 was made in each fund, the results would have been as follows:

Mutual Fund	% Gain
Selected American Shares	12.8
Boston Capital Appreciation	10.9
Stein Roe Special	9.6
Stein Roe Discovery	7.6
Selected Special Shares	6.2
Constellation Growth	5.1
Boston Special Growth	3.1
Stein Roe Capital Opportunities	− 3.2

Now you can see the value of a little study of some interesting mutual funds in advance of a first buy signal. When our data tells us that the OTC market is not safe, we can select one of the high quality funds for investment until the market leadership turns around again.

Let's review our trading results, in light of this new information. For example, let us assume that when the February 7, 1984 buy signal was flashed, we placed our investments in the Boston Capital Appreciation Fund, rather than in the Constellation Growth Fund. Also, instead of investing in the Stein Roe Capital Opportunities Fund, we shifted our purchases to the Stein Roe Special Fund. In addition, after the bull market sell signals in October 1980 and July 1983, we started the next trading cycle by investing in the higher quality funds. With these changes, our trading results would have been improved, as shown in the next two tables:

TRADING RESULTS
Constellation Growth Fund/Boston Capital Appreciation Fund

Trade Cycle	Invest	Buy NAV	Sell NAV	Sale Proceeds	Gain	Interest	New Capital
1	$10,000	6.97	7.42	$10,651	$ 651	770	$11,421
2	11,421	11.30	12.76	12,900	1,479	289	13,189
3	13,189	12.25	20.25	21,806	8,617	336	22,142
4	22,142	28.04	27.97	22,089	− 53	204	22,293
5	22,293	19.74	20.57	23,230	937	625	23,855
6	23,855	20.17	19.58	23,160	− 695	56	23,216
7	23,216	15.22	16.69	25,458	2,241	429	25,887
8	21,600	11.79	12.61	23,099	1,499	277	27,663
9	27,663	10.55	25.46	66,784	39,121	367	67,151
10	67,151	27.18	27.60	68,196	1,045	1,866	70,062
11	70,062	22.63	25.09	77,676	7,614	—	77,676

Total Gain $67,676 Percent Gain 676.8%
Percent/Year 112.5% Compounded 40.7%
Time - 6 Years

TRADING RESULTS
Stein Roe Capital Opportunities Fund/Special Fund

Trade Cycle	Invest	Buy NAV	Sell NAV	Sale Proceeds	Gain	Interest	New Capital
1	$10,000	9.81	10.88	$11,090	$ 1,245	$ 715	$11,805
2	11,805	14.47	14.95	12,199	394	144	12,343
3	12,343	14.17	23.43	20,404	8,060	324	20,728
4	20,728	14.53	14.06	20,059	− 669	206	20,265
5	20,265	21.65	22.01	20,606	341	592	21,198
6	21,198	22.08	21.56	20,694	− 504	54	20,748
7	20,748	18.85	20.20	22,228	1,480	403	22,631
8	19,000	16.35	17.53	20,369	1,369	243	24,244
9	24,244	16.01	31.56	49,419	25,175	271	49,690
10	49,690	17.12	17.09	49,599	− 91	1,345	50.944
11	50,944	13.08	14.34	55,839	4,895	—	55,839

Total Gain $45,839 Percent Gain 458.4%
Percent/Year 76.4% Compounded 33.2%
Time - 6 Years

Note: The higher quality mutual funds were used to trade cycles 4, 10 and 11.

SUMMARY

A basic system for trading no-load equity mutual funds was developed to take advantage of stock market cycles. Buy and sell rules are automatic and result in the accumulation of fund shares using a unique downward dollar cost averaging plan, combined with a trend following plan. The sell plan considers whether or not a market advance is a minor rally or the start of a new bull market. After each sell signal, the capital is returned to a money market fund to earn interest until the next trading cycle begins. A modification to the trading plan directs investments to higher quality equity funds when market conditions indicate that it is not safe to invest in OTC stocks.

During the six year period between October, 1978 and November, 1984, a trader following this system and trading two aggressive growth mutual funds would have achieved results comparable to those given in the following table:

TRADING RESULTS
Growth of Starting Capital - $10,000 Becomes:

Condition	Constellation Growth Fund		Stein Roe Capital Opportunities Fund	
	Compounded Gain		Compounded Gain	
	Capital	Gain	Capital	Gain
Basic Plan	$50,730	31.1%	$35,650	23.6%
With Interest	62,330	35.7	42,690	27.4
Switch Funds	77,680	40.7	55,840	33.2

Part II
THE GOLD MARKET

Introduction

For investment purposes, the gold market may be divided into two segments: the gold bullion market, which we are not concerned with in this work, and the stocks of gold mining companies. With the advent of mutual funds that invest in shares of gold mining companies, this area of interest has been opened to the point where even the smallest investors may participate. In general, gold mining companies are divided into South African companies and North American companies. We prefer the South African mining companies mainly because of their dividend structure. The techniques shown should work just as well for North American companies (for those investors avoiding South Africa). The companies are required by law to pay out nearly all of their earnings each year to their shareholders. This feature gives the shares considerable leverage over gold bullion, due to the potential for very high yields as the price of gold advances. Of course, the leverage factor works in both directions. Therefore, coupled with the unrest in that part of the world, trading in shares of South African mining companies has the elements of high risk as well as high rewards.

The United Services Gold Shares Fund is a no-load mutual fund that invests almost exclusively in South African gold mining companies. The fund is very widely diversified in these stocks, so that its net asset value (NAV) serves as a price index for South African mining shares, while the fund itself becomes the investment vehicle. The NAV price index will be used to calculate two moving averages which, in turn, will give the buy and sell signals.

The U.S. Gold Shares fund has been available for investment since 1974, and therefore has a price history that is over 10 years old. The fund is extremely volatile and a high level of risk must be assigned to any trading or investing methods that are undertaken. The fund's volatility stems not only from movements in the price of gold itself, but also from the anticipated effect of these movements on the dividend payout of the gold mining companies.

Because of the volatility of the fund, price changes in either direction may be extreme. In relatively short periods of time, large gains (or equally large losses) may be recorded by the fund. Therefore, the trading system that is used with the fund should be selected very carefully. The system must be defensive, with preservation of capital as the primary consideration. This indicates that a moving average trading system would most likely be satisfactory.

It will be worthwhile at this point to briefly review the price history of the fund. The U.S. Gold Shares Fund was first offered to the public in July of 1974, at a price of $5.00 per share. It then traded for about eight months with no clear upward or downward trend. In February, 1975, a sustained move to the downside started and continued relentlessly for a year and a half. The fund finally reached a low of 1.13 in August, 1976 with an incredible loss of over 73% of its net asset value. For those who bought and held from the first offering, it would now be necessary for the fund to gain over 270% just to get even! That did not happen until December of 1979, more than three years later. This type of performance certainly is a powerful argument against the buy and hold strategy for long term gains.

After the 1976 low, the NAV of the fund fluctuated in a very narrow range, between 1.30 and 1.70, for about a year. It then moved up and traded approximately between 1.70 and 2.40 until May of 1979. With this type of action, there were really no good trading opportunities during the first five years after the fund was offered to the public. Then it began to move. From an intermediate low of 2.29 in May of 1979, a great bull market developed and carried the NAV of the fund to an ultimate high of 10.53 in September of 1980. With dividends included, this is a fantastic gain of over 390%. This was during the inflationary times of the late seventies, when gold bullion reached a price of $800 an ounce. Then, as inflation began to subside, the price of gold fell steadily and the NAV of the fund plunged to 2.94, giving back most of the gains and racking up a loss of over 61%. The next bull market coincided perfectly with the bull market in stocks during 1982-1983 and yielded another huge gain of about 240%. Since that time, the fund has remained in a profitable trading range, between 5.00 and 10.00 per share.

In reviewing the historical data for the fund, it is obvious that its price movement is not cyclical. It apparently is not associated with the expansion and contraction of the economy, as stock prices are. The forces that move the price of gold, and therefore gold stocks, may stay in place for long periods of time, perhaps even for several years. Trying to find evidence to justify a bottom after a severe decline may be extremely risky and could result in considerable losses of capital. Therefore, lacking an investment model based upon indicators that have proved reliable in the past, it follows that a trading system using the more defensive nature of moving averages is an acceptable alternative. A moving average system can be relied upon to take a trader out of the market before any severe bear move can seriously erode one's capital. The problem now will be to study moving average systems, so that a safe and dependable trading program can be developed. After a suitable system is defined and tested, we will then examine some modifications which may enhance its profitability. These will include the accumulating of shares near a bottom and selling them near the top.

MOVING AVERAGES

Moving averages are generally used to establish that an uptrend or downtrend in a price index has begun. This is accomplished by noting whether the current value of the price index is above or below the average price of the index over a given period of time. The price index may be a market index, such as the Dow Jones Industrial Index, an individual stock price, or the NAV of a mutual fund. We are, of course, interested in the NAV of the U.S. Gold Shares Fund, and will use a moving average system to guide us in the purchase and sale of its shares. All references to moving averages will be to exponential moving averages, simply because they work very well and are much easier to calculate than arithmetic or front-weighted moving averages.

The basis of a moving average system is to take advantage of the fact that markets move in trends. If the moving average system indicates that an uptrend has started, we intend to move our capital into the gold fund and remain invested as long as the trend continues. When the system tells us that the trend is over, we intend to sell our shares and place our capital in a money market fund as long as the downtrend continues. In this way we hope to greatly improve upon the investment return over that obtained by merely buying and holding on.

The moving average system that we have selected was derived from an analysis of many different systems tested over the entire 10 year history of the fund. If the system worked well in the past, we will assume that it will continue to work well in the future. We will also place somewhat greater emphasis on preservation of capital than on financial gain. This is accomplished by giving up some of the early movement of a new uptrend in an effort to avoid false buy and sell signals, which almost always result in losses. Every attempt will be made to hold these losses to less than 10% of our invested capital. There is no guarantee that this can be done because of the extreme volatility of the fund. As will be seen, the final recommended system would have made only five round trip trades over the life of the fund. Four of the trades were profitable, while one gave a small loss. If the results were compounded, that is, if all dividends, capital gains and money market interest were reinvested for each trade, the starting capital of $10,000 would have grown to $118,300 over the ten year period. This return is equivalent to a very acceptable compounded annual return of 28% per year. Money market interest must be included since, with this system, we were invested in the fund only 36% of the time. An alternate system will be offered for traders who prefer more action. It will include some interesting bottom buy and top sell signals to complement the moving average system. The return was more than doubled by the inclusion of these new signals. Although the risk must be considerably higher, the increased gains would seem to adequately balance the increased risk.

In the development of any moving average trading system, there are several serious questions to consider. Some of these are:

1. Should the NAV of the fund or a short term moving average be used to flash the buy and sell signals?
2. How many days or weeks should be included in the longer moving average?
3. How can we avoid whipsaws or false buy or sell signals which almost always result in losses?
4. How do we incorporate dividend distributions made by the fund into the calculations?

Let us illustrate some of these questions with examples. Assume that we use the NAV of the fund to give signals and the value of the long term moving average is 5.00. If the NAV of the fund is 4.98 and the next day it rose to 5.02, it would give a buy signal. If, on the following day, the NAV now fell back to 4.98, this would complete a whipsaw by giving a sell signal. Signals would continue to be flashed as long as the NAV of the fund kept rising above and falling below the long term moving average. This action tells us that no clear trend has set in yet, as the NAV of the fund keeps oscillating around its moving average. The way to avoid this problem to a great extent is to use a short term moving average rather than the fund NAV itself to develop the signals. This has the effect of delaying signals until a clearer trend has started. In the research on this system, we studied the use of 5, 10, 15, 20 and 25-day short term moving averages to develop the signals. In the final recommended system, a short term moving average of 15 days is used in place of the NAV of the fund to flash the signals.

In choosing a time period for the long term moving average, there are two considerations. First, if the time period is very short, early buy signals will cause us to enter the market sooner and, if the uptrend holds, a greater proportion of the total market gain will be realized. On the other hand, entering the market too early will often put us in right at the top of a false uptrend. If the market then reverses to the downside, we will have to sell out a loss. In order to arrive at optimum conditions, the historical data was used to examine long term moving average time periods of 50, 100, 150, 200 and 250 days in combination with all of the short term moving averages. The results showed that a short term moving average of 15 days, giving signals when it crossed above or below a long term moving average of 200 days, virtually eliminated all whipsaws with little sacrifice in profits.

Before discussing the methods of calculation, let us review the trading results which led us to the final recommended moving average system. The very worst trading system that used two moving averages came from the combination of 5 days and 50 days. Over the 10 year period, there were a total of 44 round trip trades. Of these, 17 gave profits and 27 gave losses. Total trading profits were only about half those achieved with the optimum system. Impossible situations frequently arose, when buy and sell signals were given on successive days. Most investors do not care to be this active and the fund itself also tries to discourage excessive trading. Any system should work within the rather lenient restrictions of the U.S. Gold Shares Fund, which permits 12 exchanges in any 12 month period at a modest charge of $5.00 per exchange. After 12 exchanges in 12 months, the charge increases to $50.00 per exchange. A long term moving average of 50 days is simply unacceptable.

The most profitable combination of two moving averages was 5 days and 150 days, which gave a total of 17 round trip trades. Four of these would be classified as whipsaws that required a round trip to be completed in just a few days. This system would probably be satisfactory for an experienced trader who could use his good judgment to employ some type of filter to avoid the whipsaws. Even so, this combination was only slightly more profitable than the combination of 15 days and 200 days.

The 15-day moving average crossing the 200-day moving average was easily the most productive system that could be discovered. Taking a capsule look at the historical NAV data for the fund, we see that there were two long term bear markets and two long term bull markets. Any system that simply kept us out of the bear moves and put us into the bull moves produced excellent results. The 15-day/200-day combination did exactly that. The system does demand a lot of patience, as there were no trades during the first 31 months after the fund was offered for sale. During that time, the fund was losing some 70% of its value. After two minor gains in 1977 and 1978, the bull market of 1979 returned a profit of over 300%. The system then took us out of the fund for three more years, after which it put us in again in 1982 for another gain of 64%. A short cycle in 1984 resulted in a loss of 1.7%, the only loss encountered to date. Charts showing the NAV of the fund, the 15-day moving average and the 200-day moving average have been constructed for the entire 10 year history of the fund and are included in the Appendix. It is worth studying these charts to see how well the moving average system worked during long uptrends and downtrends. We will also make use of the charts later, when we develop modifications to the trading system.

When the fund declares a dividend distribution to shareholders and goes x-dividend by removing the amount of the dividend from the assets of the fund, the result is an unwarranted drop in the NAV. If this drop is not accounted for in the calculations, a false buy or sell signal could be triggered. The problem has been resolved by adjusting the fund NAV for the distribution before making the moving average calculations. This is done by removing only 1/100th of the dividend each day for the next 100 days after the fund has gone x-dividend. In this way, the effect of the distribution is added very gradually. It also permits continuity in the calculations without the necessity to go back over the data and adjust the NAV values for the distribution. Any effect of the dividend on buy and sell signals will be spread out over a period of 100 days, and will therefore be insignificant. For those investors who prefer to plot the moving average data on graphs, the adjusted data may be used and it is then not necessary to replot the data.

77

Part II—The Gold Market

CALCULATIONS

The method for calculation of exponential moving averages was presented in detail in an earlier chapter. Only a brief review will be given here. At any point in time, our worksheet will look something like this:

Date	NAV	Dividend	Adjusted NAV	15-Day EA	200-Day EA
8/12/81	6.03	.0000	6.0300	5.672	6.520
8/13/81	6.12	.0000	6.1200	5.728	6.516
8/14/81	5.73	.3900	6.1200	5.777	6.512
8/17/81	5.81	.3861	6.1961	5.829	6.509
8/18/81	6.13	.3822	6.5122	5.914	6.509
8/19/81	6.11	.3783	6.4883	5.986	6.508

The above sample data shows that on August 14, the fund made a dividend distribution of 39 cents per share. Note also that the NAV of the fund dropped exactly .39 from the day before. The entire decline was therefore due to the payment of the dividend, which was removed from the assets of the fund. In order to prevent the large decline in the NAV from seriously affecting the moving averages, especially the short term moving average, it is necessary to make an adjustment to the NAV. This is done by removing just 1/100th of the dividend, or .0039, from the NAV each day for 100 days. The above table illustrates how this is done. The fourth column, headed "Adjusted NAV," has the dividend added back. After 100 days, the entire amount of the distribution will have been removed and the NAV and the adjusted NAV will be identical. The adjusted NAV is used to calculate the two exponential moving averages.

The moving averages are calculated with the aid of a "smoothing constant" which gives a result that is almost equivalent to an arithmetic moving average. The smoothing constant is calculated as follows:

$$\text{Constant} = \frac{2}{(N + 1)}$$

where N is the number of data points or days in the moving average. The smoothing constant for the 15-day exponential average is 2 divided by 16 or .125. For the 200-day average it is 2 divided by 201 or .01. The 15-day EA is calculated from the equation:

$$\text{Exp. Avg.} = (NAV \times .125) + (EA \times (1 - .125))$$
$$= (NAV \times .125) + (EA \times .875)$$

where,

Exp. Avg. = new or today's exponential average
EA = last or yesterday's exponential average

The 200-day EA is calculated in the same way, using .01 for the smoothing constant. Remember that it will require 200 days of calculations for the moving average to be completely valid. There are several ways to obtain the old data needed to do these calculations. You may write to the fund and request the NAV data for the past year. The data may also be obtained from back copies of almost any newspaper at the local library. It would also be satisfactory to obtain weekly NAV data from back issues of Barron's at the library and calculate an exponential average for the past 40 weeks. The result would be nearly equivalent to a 200-day average. The address of the fund is:

United Services Gold Shares, Inc.
Box 29467
San Antonio, TX 78229

If it is inconvenient to make these simple calculations on a daily basis, there is no reason that the data could not be saved until the weekend and, in a few minutes, the worksheet for the entire week may be filled in. Buy and sell signals occur so rarely, there would be no problem. If a signal is forthcoming, the worksheet could then be kept on a daily basis. The buy and sell rules are very simple—buy when the 15-day moving average crosses above the 200-day moving average; sell when the 15-day moving average crosses below the 200-day moving average.

The following table gives the investment results in summary form. It covers the ten year time period from December 31, 1974 to December 31, 1984. The plan assumes that starting capital of $10,000 was placed in a money market fund on January 1, 1975 and that telephone exchanges would permit the purchase or sale of fund shares on the day following each buy or sell signal. It further assumes that all interest, dividends and capital gain distributions were reinvested so that all gains were compounded. Fund shares were purchased with all available capital when the 15-day moving average crossed above the 200-day moving average. All shares were sold when the 15-day moving average crossed below the 200-day moving average. Money market interest rates were assumed to be equal to the rate on 91-day Treasury Bills. Using this method for trading, it can be seen that the starting capital of $10,000 would have grown to $118,387 over the 10 year period. This was equivalent to a compounded annual return of 28% per year, a very satisfying result and a reward for patience, since, as it turned out, shares of the fund were owned just 36% of the time. Therefore, the money market interest was an important contribution to the profitability of the system. For comparison, if the $10,000 starting capital had been used to buy shares of the fund at the start of the period and held throughout, it would have grown to just $24,430, even with all distributions reinvested. The compounded annual return would have been just 9.3% per year.

TRADING RESULTS
United Services Gold Shares Fund
With Money Market Interest

Trade	Invest	Buy NAV	Sell NAV	Sale Proceeds	Gain	Interest	New Capital
—	—	—	—	—	—	$ 1,805	$ 11,805
1	$ 11,805	1.57	1.72	$ 12,927	$ 1,122	140	13,067
2	13,067	1.85	1.87	13,175	108	292	13,467
3	13,467	1.80	7.39	55,324	41,857	12,249	67,573
4	67,573	4.52	7.42	110,885	43,312	3,280	114,165
5	114,165	8.12	7.98	112,197	− 1,968	6,190	118,387

Total Gain $108,387   Percent Gain 1,083.9%
Percent/Year 108.3%   Compounded 28.0%
Time - 10 Years

MODIFYING THE SYSTEM

The Gold trading system that has just been presented is a relatively simple system that flashes buy signals when the 15-day exponential moving average (EA) crosses above the 200-day EA and sell signals when the crossing is reversed. In the event that a false buy signal is given, that is, one that is followed by a reversal of the market to the downside, we will be taken out of the market by the oncoming sell signal. If a loss develops from this particular sequence, it is usually a small one. We have also seen that those investors who are using a buy and hold system could have bought in at the top of a long and severe bear market. It would then be their misfortune to hold the position for years before they see a profit or just get even. Many investors do not have the fortitude or the patience to hold through long bear markets and are forced to sell out only after they have suffered disastrous losses. Some investors follow a dollar cost averaging program and continue to purchase more shares each month at lower and lower prices. However, they will find that very soon their new purchases have practically no effect on the average price they have paid for each share. Their losses will also continue to mount and they will have a long wait before they get even or can show a profit.

There is also the opposite situation to consider. Suppose an investor, using either the buy and hold system or the dollar cost averaging system, is fortunate enough to start his program right at the beginning of a long bull market. After seeing the investment grow into a large paper profit, the question now becomes one of when to sell. As we have seen, a profit of 50%, 100%, or even more than 200% would be possible. Should the investor continue to hold and keep buying more shares? Between May of 1979 and September of 1980, the U.S. Gold Shares Fund advanced from 2.29 per share to 10.53 per share, for a gain of over 390%. By June of 1982, the NAV of the fund had fallen back to 2.94. The investors who held on through these cycles had to watch all of those generous profits simply disappear. It is just as important to know when to sell as it is to know when to buy, as this type of performance certainly demonstrates.

The modified system that will now be presented will take the best features from both the moving average trading system and the dollar cost averaging system and combine them with a new sell plan. This modified trading system will greatly increase the potential for generating profits. All questions concerning when to buy or when to sell will be eliminated. The new system will require only one more calculation to be added to the worksheet.

The profit potential for the new system is extremely high. Even though we all understand that past performance does not predict the future, we have only the past data to examine. In any event, $10,000 placed in the system on January 1, 1975 with all dividends, interest and capital gains reinvested, would have grown to over $240,000 in ten years, for a compounded annual return of over 37%. The potential for these gains has not changed. Inflationary expectations may return at any time, causing the price of gold to advance. These movements may develop into long term trends. An investor who has positioned himself in the market very early may realize these gains again. The risks are high, especially with the current political problems in South Africa. Certainly, only a small percentage of anyone's assets should be earmarked for this type of speculation.

First, look again at the moving average graphs in the Appendix. Starting in August, 1975 and continuing for about a year, we see that the NAV of the fund, followed closely by the 15-day EA, was far below the 200-day EA. This was the result of a severe bear market taking place at that time. A similar performance was seen again during the first six months of 1982. Would it not be wise to begin a "downward" dollar cost averaging program when we recognize that we are well into a severe downtrend? It would not be the usual monthly purchase program however, as it would be our intention to make more purchases only if the market continued its decline. In other words, we would plan to make our first purchase only when the market acquired sufficient downward momentum to give promise of further declines. Subsequent purchases would be made only if the market continued to decline by a predetermined amount. In this way the reality of the downward cost averaging program would be assured.

It now must be determined when to make the first purchase and what minimum decline is required for subsequent purchases. Downward momentum may be measured by calculating the percent difference between the 15-day EA and the 200-day EA. In the severe bear market of 1975, the 15-day EA fell as much as 33% below the 200-day EA. However, in other bear markets, the difference was not much greater than − 20%. Therefore, to have a fair chance to participate in this type of downward cost averaging, it would be reasonable to make a first purchase when the 15-day EA declined to 20% below the 200-day EA. With the possibility of a severe further decline in the future, we should commit only about 20% of our starting capital for the first purchase. This will leave us with adequate remaining capital for future purchases at much lower prices.

We have not abandoned our basic moving average trading program. If the market now were to reverse to the upside, with a crossing of the moving averages, we would then commit all of our remaining capital on this major buy signal. However, if the market continued to decline, we would plan to make additional purchases at greatly lower prices. If the NAV of the fund were to drop another 20% from its value on the day of the first buy signal, we would make a second purchase with another 20% of our original capital. Let it be clear that the first buy signal is flashed when the 15-day EA declines at least 20% below the 200-day EA. The second buy signal is given only when the NAV of the fund declines another 20% below its value on the day of the first buy signal. After the first buy signal is given, the percent difference between the two moving averages is of no further consequence in the program. If desired, its calculation can be omitted from the worksheet until the 15-day EA crosses above the 200-day EA.

If the market were to continue its decline, additional purchases with 20% of our starting capital would be made each time the NAV of the fund fell another 20% from the last buy point. There is some possibility that the bear market would be so severe and so extended that a total of five buy signals would be flashed. However, that would require a decline in the fund NAV of at least 60-70% to complete.

If the fund were to make a dividend distribution at any time after a buy signal has been given, it is only necessary to subtract the amount of the dividend from the next buy point. For example, if the next buy point was calculated to be 5.75 and the fund went x-dividend for 23 cents, the next buy point would be lowered to 5.52. Other buy points would be lowered accordingly.

The percent difference between the 15-day EA and the 200-day EA is calculated using the standard percent equation:

$$\text{Percent} = \frac{(\text{EA 15} - \text{EA 200}) \times 100}{\text{EA 200}}$$

To take a closer look at how the buy program works in practice, we will examine the data for the U.S. Gold Shares Fund and its moving averages around the time of the July, 1981 buy signal. After adding another column to the worksheet to record the percent difference between the two moving averages, the data would have looked like this at the time of the first signal:

Date	NAV	Dividend	Adjusted NAV	EA 15	EA200	Percent Difference
6/26/81	5.04	0	5.040	5.658	6.900	− 18.0
6/29/81	4.82	0	4.820	5.553	6.879	− 19.3
6/30/81	4.98	0	4.980	5.481	6.860	− 20.1
7/ 1/81	4.93	0	4.930	5.412	6.841	− 20.9
7/ 2/81	5.06	0	5.060	5.363	6.823	− 21.3

On June 30, the 15-day moving average declined to a point where it was 20.1% below the 200-day EA and therefore triggered the first buy signal. The NAV of the fund was 4.98. This value was used to calculate the remaining four buy points as follows:

$$\text{Buy } 2 = 4.98 \times .80 = 3.98$$
$$\text{Buy } 3 = 3.98 \times .80 = 3.19$$
$$\text{Buy } 4 = 3.19 \times .80 = 2.55$$
$$\text{Buy } 5 = 2.55 \times .80 = 2.04$$

On the June 30 buy signal, we would have purchased shares of the fund with 20% of our available capital by making a telephone exchange from the money market fund or by making a telephone purchase, assuming that we had previously opened our account. The purchase price on July 1 was 4.93 per share.

On August 14, the fund went x-dividend in the amount of 39 cents, with the NAV of the fund at 5.73. It was now necessary to calculate new buy points by subtracting .39 from each of the above values:

$$\text{Buy } 2 = 3.98 - .39 = 3.59$$
$$\text{Buy } 3 = 3.19 - .39 = 2.80$$
$$\text{Buy } 4 = 2.55 - .39 = 2.16$$
$$\text{Buy } 5 = 2.04 - .39 = 1.65$$

This adjustment is made to the buy points because the removal of a dividend from the NAV of the fund does not represent a decline in its market value. The amount of the dividend is paid to each shareholder. If elected by the shareholder, the total amount of the dividend may be reinvested in new shares rather than taken in cash. Anyone interested in maximum capital gains would make this choice. The payment of the dividend at a price of 5.73 reduced our average price per share from 4.93 to 4.62.

The NAV of the fund fluctuated in a rather narrow range for the next six months and no new signals were forthcoming. On January 22, 1982, the fund went x-dividend again for 25 cents. Again we adjusted our remaining buy points downward by the same amount, and the second buy point was now reduced to 3.34. The dividend was reinvested in new shares and had the effect of lowering the average price paid for each share from 4.62 to 4.37. The fund NAV now began to decline again, and on March 8 it closed at 3.32, triggering the second buy signal. The purchase was made the next day with 20% of our original capital at a price of 3.48 per share. The average price paid for each share was now reduced to 3.87 with this purchase. The Buy 3 point was now 2.55, but this value was not to be seen in this cycle. The fund made its low on June 21, and then began a strong advance. On August 13, the fund again went x-dividend for 19 cents per share, lowering the average price paid per share to 3.70. On August 24, the advance finally carried the 15-day EA above the 200-EA, triggering a major moving average buy signal. All remaining capital was used to purchase shares the next day at 4.72 per share. The crossing of the moving averages completed the buying phase using the modified system.

After the final purchase had been made, the effect of the downward cost averaging could be seen. By dividing the total amount of capital invested in the fund by the total number of shares owned, the average price per share can be calculated. During this sequence, the average price was found to be 4.20 per share. This was significantly below the 4.72 per share we would have paid if we had waited for the moving average crossing.

A disadvantage of the new system is that we may enter the market long before the moving average signal is given and as the market continues to decline, we must hold our shares while looking at increasing paper losses. Some money market interest will be lost, but should be offset by dividend distributions. The one great advantage is that we have invested our capital at a greatly reduced average price per share.

THE MODIFIED SELL PLAN

One of the drawbacks of a moving average trading system is that a buy signal is not given until the market has already undergone a considerable advance and, similarly, a sell signal is not flashed until the market has declined to a point far below its last high point. The addition of buy signals based on the downward cost averaging concept described in the last chapter helps overcome the bottom buy problem. Now we will work out a plan to improve the efficiency of the sell signals.

A good illustration of the difficulty with the sell signal can be seen by turning once again to the graphs found in the Appendix. Look at the end of the 1979-1980 bull market. On September 22, 1980, the NAV of the fund reached 10.53, the ultimate bull market high. The moving average sell signal was not given until January 21, 1981, when the shares were sold for 7.39, some 30% below the high.

If we examine the chart formations during the bull markets, we note that there are times when powerful advances carry the NAV of the fund and the 15-day EA far above the 200-day EA. When this happens, there is likely to be a short correction. This may carry the 15-day EA back down fairly near to the 200-day EA.

This process may be repeated several times in a long bull market. The percent difference between the 15-day EA and the 200-day EA is now a part of our daily worksheet, so let us look at the extreme high values that have been reached in these bull markets and also the low value in the correction that followed. The first peak in the 15-day EA was recorded on October 2, 1979, when it rose to a point that was 32.9% above the 200-day EA. It then fell back to a low of + 19.4% on November 2nd. If we continue to examine these peaks and their correction values, we come up with the following:

Date	High	Date	Low
10/ 1/79	+ 32.9	11/ 2/79	+ 19.4
1/21/80	+ 54.4	4/ 6/80	+ 12.4
7/29/80	+ 32.4	8/19/81	+ 26.8
9/23/80	+ 46.9	1/21/81	0
10/22/81	+ 26.0	11/22/82	+ 14.5
1/19/83	+ 45.8	3/31/82	+ 8.9
5/18/83	+ 25.7	10/ 3/83	0

The low value of 0 indicates that the 15-day EA crossed below the 200-day EA, giving a major moving average sell signal. There were three occasions when the percent difference rose above + 45%, with the correction that followed taking the difference back down below + 15%. These were the points of interest. Let's assume that when the 15-day EA rises more than 45% above the 200-day EA there is likely to be a rather sharp correction. It would make sense to sell out at or near the peak, with the intention of buying back after the correction carried the market down to a point lower than about + 15%. This would amount to a "rollover;" that is, selling at a high point and repurchasing at a lower point. It is important to repurchase the shares after the correction, since there is no reason to believe that the bull market is over—it just needs a rest from the extreme upside action and has become excessively overbought. Technically, the 200-day EA often acts as a strong support level, a point where new buying will come into the market and reverse the downtrend. In a bull market, investors and traders alike often wait for a downward correction, so that they can enter the market somewhat below its last intermediate high point. In effect, a rollover would permit us to sell high and buy low, all within the context of an ongoing bull market. This action has the potential to enhance our profits considerably. In fact, in the 1979-1980 bull market, the use of the rollover plan would have increased our capital by more than 50% compared to the gains achieved by the straight moving average system.

There is a possible complication that may well arise when attempting to use the rollover program. What if the market does not correct down to a +15% before turning around and continuing its advance? There are two courses of action that may be considered. One is to simply ignore the market at that point, especially if the profits from the sale were very substantial. We may fail to increase our profits from that point, but there will be no losses and our money will be safely placed in a money market fund awaiting some future opportunity. The other choice would be to buy in as soon as it became clear that the downward correction was over, as signalled by a change in direction of the percent difference between the two moving averages. A repurchase at any price below the last sell point is sure to yield a higher overall profit than the straight moving average trading system itself, and the money market interest earned in the interim could be substantial.

We will now develop a set of buy and sell rules using the moving average trading system combined with the special bottom buy and top sell modifications. The worksheet will show the fund NAV, along with any adjustment required for dividend distributions, the 15-day EA, the 200-day EA and the percent difference between them.

BUY AND SELL RULES

Buy Rules

1. Buy shares in the U.S. Gold Shares Fund with 100% of capital any time the 15-day EA crosses above the 200-day EA.

2. Buy shares in the fund with 20% of available capital when the 15-day EA declines at least 20% below the 200-day EA. The NAV of the fund on this date is the Buy 1 point.

3. Buy shares in the fund with 20% of starting capital when the NAV declines to a value that is 80% of the Buy 1 point. The NAV of the fund on this date is the Buy 2 point.

4. Buy shares in the fund with 20% of starting capital when the NAV declines to a value that is 80% of the Buy 2 point. The NAV of the fund on this date is the Buy 3 point.

5. Continue buying shares with 20% of capital each time the NAV declines by 20% from the previous buy point, until all capital is invested. Hold the shares until a sell signal is received.

6. If all shares were sold according to Sell Rule 2 below, buy back shares with all available capital as soon as the 15-day EA declines from its high point to a value that is just less than 15% *above* the 200-day EA.

Sell Rules

1. Sell all shares when the 15-day EA crosses below the 200-day EA.

2. Sell all shares when the 15-day EA rises 45% above the 200-day EA.

Note: If the fund goes x-dividend, the amount of the distribution must be subtracted from all buy points not yet executed.

TRADING SIGNALS

Having developed a set of buy and sell rules to cover the modifications to the trading system, the historical NAV data of the fund was processed to show each buy and sell signal as it occurred. There are a total of only eight round trip trades during the ten years. The first cycle covered a period of time from September, 1975 to April, 1978, some two and one-half years. While this was the exception rather than the rule, sometimes a great deal of patience is required. The complete list of trading signals, along with any action taken as a result of the signals, is given in the following tables.

TRADING SIGNALS

A Summary of all Buy and Sell Signals that Required Some Action While Trading the United Services Gold Shares Fund.

Date	Signal
9/18/75	NAV = 3.01. 15-day EA is 20.7% below 200-day EA. Purchase shares of the fund with 20% of starting capital. Next buy point = 2.41, a 20% decline in the fund NAV.
11/18/75	NAV = 2.40, buy shares with 20% of starting capital. Next buy point = 1.93.
3/ 8/76	Dividend = .05. Next buy point = 1.88.
3/29/76	NAV = 1.79, buy shares with 20% of starting capital. Next buy point = 1.49.
8/ 2/76	NAV = 1.46, buy shares with 20% of starting capital. Next buy point = 1.18.
8/23/76	NAV = 1.15, buy shares with all remaining capital. Now fully invested.
7/25/77	15-day EA = 1.573, 200-day EA = 1.569. Moving average buy signal. No action required as we are fully invested.
4/17/78	15-day EA = 1.928, 200-day EA = 1.939. Moving average sell signal. Sell all shares.
6/ 9/78	NAV = 1.93, 15-day EA = 1.913, 200-day EA = 1.910. Moving average buy signal. Buy shares of the fund with all available capital.

TRADING SIGNALS (Cont'd)

Date	Signal
11/ 2/78	NAV = 1.91, 15-day EA = 2.079, 200-day EA = 2.093. Sell signal. Sell all shares.
1/24/79	NAV = 2.14, 15-day EA = 2.028, 200-day EA = 2.012. Moving average buy signal. Buy shares of the fund with all available capital.
1/15/80	NAV = 6.26, 15-day EA = 5.285, 200-day EA 3.577. 15-day EA is 47.7% above the 200-day EA. Top sell signal. Sell all shares.
4/ 1/80	NAV = 4.69, 15-day EA = 5.516, 200-day EA = 4.517. 15-day EA is 14.1% above 200-day EA. Buy signal. Buy shares with all available capital.
9/19/80	NAV = 10.53, 15-day EA = 9.272, 200-day EA = 6.392. 15-day EA is 45.1% above 200-day EA. Top sell signal. Sell all shares.
12/15/80	NAV = 8.51, 15-day EA = 8.963, 200-day EA = 7.811. 15-day EA is 14.7% above 200-day EA. Buy signal. Buy shares with all available capital.
1/20/81	NAV = 7.38, 15-day EA = 7.814, 200-day EA = 7.870. Moving average sell signal. Sell all shares.
6/30/81	NAV = 4.98, 15-day EA = 5.481, 200-day EA = 6.860. 15-day EA is 20.1% below 200-day EA. Buy signal. Buy shares with 20% of starting capital. Next buy point = 3.98.
8/14/81	Dividend = .39, next buy point = 3.59.
1/22/82	Dividend = .25, next buy point = 3.34.
3/ 8/82	NAV = 3.32, buy shares with 20% of starting capital. Next buy point = 2.67.
8/24/82	NAV = 4.59, 15-day EA = 4.412, 200-day EA = 4.381. Moving average buy signal. Buy shares with all remaining capital.

TRADING SIGNALS (Cont'd)

Date	Signal
1/17/83	NAV = 8.92, 15-day EA = 8.537, 200-day EA = 5.869. 15-day EA is 45.5% above the 200-day EA. Top sell signal. Sell all shares.
3/21/83	NAV = 7.19, 15-day EA = 7.744, 200-day EA = 6.776. 15-day EA is 14.3% above the 200-day EA. Buy signal. Buy shares with all available capital.
10/ 3/83	NAV = 7.12, 15-day EA = 8.313, 200-day EA = 8.333. Moving average sell signal. Sell all shares.
2/16/84	NAV = 8.08, 15-day EA = 7.815, 200-day EA = 7.766. Moving average buy signal. Buy shares with all available capital.
6/27/84	NAV = 7.90, 15-day EA = 8.243, 200-day EA = 8.267. Moving average sell signal. Sell all shares.

TRADING RESULTS

The following table gives the trading results that would have been achieved if the buy and sell rules had been followed without exception, and we had acted on each signal given in the previous tables. The time period covered is ten years, ending on June 30, 1984. The trading program assumes that starting capital was $10,000 and that purchases and sales were made on the day following the signals. All interest, dividends and trading profits were reinvested, so that all gains were compounded. Money market interest rates were assumed to be equal to the rate on 91-day Treasury Bills. Following this program, the starting capital of $10,000 would have grown to almost $250,000, for an annual compounded gain of 38.0% per year, truly an outstanding result.

TRADING RESULTS

United Services Gold Shares Fund
With Money Market Interest Modified System

Trade	Invest	Buy NAV	Sell NAV	Sale Proceeds	Capital Gain	Interest	New Capital
—	—	—	—	—	—	$ 903	$ 10,903
1	$ 10,903	1.53	1.72	$ 12,262	$ 1,359	130	12,392
2	12,392	1.84	1.87	12,625	234	288	12,913
3	12,913	1.96	6.22	41,028	28,115	1,204	42,232
4	42,232	4.55	10.25	95,163	52,931	2,891	98,054
5	98,054	8.12	7.39	89,239	− 8,815	16,652	105,891
6	105,891	4.20	8.90	224,704	118,813	1,116	225,820
7	225,820	7.10	7.42	235,959	10,139	6,131	242,090
8	242,090	8.12	7.98	237,916	− 4,174	12,070	249,986

Total Gain $239,986 Percent Gain 2,400%
Percent/Year 240% Compounded 38.0%
Time - 10 Years

Part III
THE BOND MARKET

Introduction

Trading in corporate, municipal or government bonds bears almost no relationship to trading in stocks. Bond prices move up or down inversely with interest rates; that is, when interest rates decline, bond prices rise and when interest rates rise, bond prices decline. Therefore, purchases of bonds should be limited to periods of falling interest rates, regardless of the yields paid on the bonds. Investments in bonds during periods of rising interest rates will result in a loss of capital which may or may not be recovered by the interest payments on the bonds.

A study of bond prices over the past eight years has shown that they tend to move in one direction or the other for extended periods of time. This price action suggests that a moving average crossing system would be suitable for trading bonds. If so, it would be necessary to develop an appropriate bond index, whose moving average could be used to give buy and sell signals for trading. Selection of a bond mutual fund for trading is not difficult, since almost every mutual fund family offers one or more bond funds, all of which are very similar.

Trading in bonds gives one the opportunity to enhance interest income from capital that is normally kept in money market funds or bank certificates of deposit. Conservative investors will find bonds to be an attractive, low risk alternative to investing in the stock market. During times of declining interest rates, capital may be moved into a bond fund where a high yield is virtually locked in. If the timing is good and interest rates continue to fall, a capital gain will result when the bond fund is eventually sold. The use of a moving average trend following system greatly reduces the risk of loss. The bond fund will simply be sold if the market moves against us. The trading system will limit any loss to less than 3% of capital, much of which may be recovered by the interest earned. I personally feel that the risk is so low that all investors willing to do the minimal daily arithmetic required to develop the signals should take advantage of the trading system. Those who need the interest income to cover living expenses will find that the continual increase in capital gains will greatly enhance that income. The trading system is also an excellent alternative for IRA accounts, which ordinarily are placed in bank certificates of deposit.

The moving average trading system that will be presented is more profitable than might be expected at first. The system was tested over the five year period beginning January 1, 1980 and ending December 31, 1984. It was assumed that starting capital was $10,000. On each buy signal, it was exchanged to the Fidelity High Income Bond Fund. On each sell signal, all capital was placed back in the Fidelity Cash Reserves money market fund. In the first case, all dividends, interest and capital gains were kept in the system and reinvested with each buy signal. This would be the standard procedure for an IRA program. At the end of the five year period, it had grown to $28,590, for a compounded annual return of over 23.3%. This is certainly an excellent return for investing in the relative safety of bonds. In the second case, it was assumed that all distributions were taken in cash but that any capital gains were reinvested. This program is recommended for those investors who would prefer to receive the interest in cash, but would also like to have the opportunity for capital gains. Without capital gains, the effects of inflation could erode your capital. In this case the starting capital grew to $15,000, for a compounded annual return of 8.6%. This rate of return would seem adequate to counteract the effects of inflation while continuously increasing the income available from their capital.

BOND INDICES

One of the few widely available bond indices that can be used to determine the direction of bond prices is the Dow Jones 20 Bond Index. This index is widely published and can be found in most local newspapers. The index is composed of 10 corporate bonds and 10 utility bonds. There are relatively few issues in the index, so it was determined, after much experimentation, that the index is simply not broad enough to be a reliable indicator for the prices of all bonds traded on the New York Bond Exchange. It was necessary to devise a second index to be used in conjunction with the 20 Bond Index to develop the signals. This latter index is called the advance/decline (A/D) bond index, and is a simple arithmetic total of the daily advances and declines in prices of all bonds traded on the exchange. One difficulty with this index is that the data needed is available only in good financial publications such as the Wall Street Journal, New York Times, or Barron's, a weekly financial publication. These two bond indices are used together to determine the price movement of bonds and to give the buy and sell signals.

The trading system is based upon the 25-day exponential moving averages of the two indices. Buy signals are given when both indices cross above their 25-day EA's, and sell signals are given when both indices cross below them. There is just one modification. When a buy signal is given and the market turns down, so that both indices fall below their 25-day EA's, the bond fund shares are not sold immediately but are held until the NAV of the fund declines at least 2% below the buy point. This will give the market time to resume its upward trend in some cases and prevent unwanted whipsaws. In other cases, we will be forced to sell out as the market continues to decline. In that event, our losses will be limited to the range of 2%. The great problem with any moving average system is the occurrence of whipsaws. These happen when the market turns down right after a buy signal or turns up after a sell signal. The use of a 2% stop-loss sell point will greatly reduce the number of whipsaws while protecting our capital from large losses. If the bond market firms and advances as expected, the stop-loss sell point is cancelled when the NAV of the fund rises 2% above the buy point.

BOND MUTUAL FUNDS

It is highly recommended that only no-load bond mutual funds be used for trading. Almost all families of mutual funds offer a variety of bond funds which can be traded successfully with this system. All of the fund families also have money market funds where trading capital may be kept, earning high rates of interest while waiting for the next buy signal to develop. It is most important that the funds permit exchanges between the bond fund and the money market fund and that these exchanges can be arranged by telephone. Some fund families permit telephone exchanges, but only after investments in the funds have been on deposit for 30, 60 or even 90 days. When calling for a prospectus, inquire about any restrictions associated with telephone exchanges. There are many good bond funds available without these restrictions. Don't be encumbered by unnecessary delays. Other fund families limit the number of exchanges that may be made with one fund in one year, but these are usually reasonable limits. If a fund allows even three round trip exchanges per year, that should be adequate. We do not expect that high a trading frequency with the system. During the five year test period, there were just 10 round trip trades, with not more than three in any one year.

The great advantage of no-load mutual funds is the immediate and widespread diversification provided for investments, regardless of the dollar amount. There are also no commissions or sales charges incurred when capital is exchanged between funds. A good choice for a trading vehicle is a high yield corporate bond fund. This type of fund has a portfolio of lower rated but higher yielding bonds. Safety is maintained because investments by the fund are broadly diversified over a great number of corporations. Professional management also insures that unnecessary risks are avoided. Interest rate yields will be about 1% to 2% higher than with bond funds that invest only in top quality corporate or government bonds. The risk is minimal, even though recent reference to "junk bonds," as they are sometimes called, has been in the news because a rash of these high yielding bonds were issued to raise capital for corporate takeovers. For those who prefer a more conservative approach, the system will work equally well with high quality corporate bond funds, GNMA funds, government bond funds, limited term bond funds or even tax-free municipal bond funds.

CALCULATIONS

The bond trading system requires the calculation of two 25-day exponential moving averages—the Dow Jones 20 Bond Index and the A/D Bond Index. The smoothing constant for a 25-day EA is 2 divided by 26, or 0.08. The data must be collected for a period of at least 25 days before the moving averages are completely valid. The initial A/D Bond Index may be set at any convenient number, such as 10,000 or 50,000. This eliminates the necessity of working with negative numbers in the event that the next move for the bond market is downward. If the index goes over 100,000, one zero can be dropped, setting the index back to 10,000. The actual magnitude of the A/D index is not meaningful. It is only the relationship between the index and its moving average that is important. The 25-day EA is calculated by means of the following equation:

$$\text{25-Day EA} = (\text{Index} \times .08) + (\text{EA} \times .92)$$

where,

$$\text{Index} = \text{latest value of the index}$$
$$\text{EA} = \text{previous exponential average}$$

101

Example:

$$A/D \text{ Index} = 44{,}266$$
$$\text{Previous EA} = 44{,}798$$

therefore,

$$
\begin{aligned}
\text{25-Day EA} &= (44{,}266 \times .08) + (44{,}798 \times .92) \\
&= 3541 + 41{,}214 \\
&= 44{,}755
\end{aligned}
$$

If the data had been kept on a daily basis during July of 1984, our worksheet would have looked like this:

Date	20 Bond Index	.08 EA	Advances	Declines	A/D Index	.08 EA	Remarks
1984							
7/ 6	64.85	65.41	227	353	44112	44798	
7/ 9	65.11	65.39	426	272	44266	44755	
7/10	65.43	65.39	416	276	44406	44727	Buy alert!
7/11	65.22	65.38	317	348	44375	44699	Cancel
7/12	65.22	65.36	391	243	44523	44685	
7/13	65.41	65.37	434	209	44748	44690	Buy signal
7/16	65.61	65.39	424	250	44922	44709	
7/17	65.58	65.40	337	340	44919	44726	

Looking at the table, we see that on July 10th the 20 Bond Index moved above its 25-day EA, but this crossing was not confirmed by the A/D Index. However, we were now alerted to the possibility of a buy signal. The next day the 20 Bond Index fell back below its EA and therefore the alert was cancelled. Just two days later, both indices moved above their moving averages and gave a buy signal. The bond purchase was made on Monday, July 16th by calling the fund and requesting that an exchange be made from the money market fund to the bond fund.

To illustrate how the stop-loss sell plan works, let us assume that we had purchased the Fidelity High Income Fund on July 16th at 8.10 per share. We now calculated a sell point that was 2% below this value, or 7.94. In the event that the market turned down and the indices fell back below their moving averages, we would not sell immediately but would wait until the NAV of the fund actually fell below our stop-loss point of 7.94. This action is required in order to prevent whipsaws. The market has shown strength, as the indices have moved up above their moving averages, but occasionally it needs to consolidate before the advance can continue. In the above example, after the July buy signal there was some retrenchment, and on July 23 both indices fell below their 25-day EA's. No action was required since we were now using our stop-loss sell point to determine when to sell. The High Income Fund was steady, with the NAV at 8.08, which proved to be the low point in this cycle. The next day, both indices advanced back above their EA's as the bond market began a strong advance. On August 2nd, the NAV of the fund reached 8.29, which was more than 2% above the buy point. This action automatically cancelled the stop-loss sell point. Once the fund advances by 2% above its buy point, the next sell signal is given in the normal way, by a downward crossing of the indices below their moving averages. Actually, the next sell signal was not flashed until February 26, 1985 with the fund NAV at 8.80. This example illustrates how the use of the stop-sell point avoided an unnecessary whipsaw as the two indices fell below their 25-day EA's for just one day shortly after the buy signal was given.

During the course of the five year test period, there were just 10 round trip transactions. A buy signal was given when both the Dow Jones 20 Bond Index and the A/D Index crossed their 25-day exponential moving averages to the upside. A sell signal was given when both indices crossed their moving averages to the downside. After each buy signal, a stop-loss sell point was calculated. This was 2% below the buy point. In the event that the market reversed to the downside after a buy signal, the bond fund was sold only if the stop-sell point was penetrated. When the NAV of the fund rose 2% above the buy point, the stop-loss point was cancelled. The following tables list each buy and sell signal that was encountered during the five years between January, 1980 and December, 1984 while trading between the Fidelity High Income Bond Fund and the Fidelity Cash Reserves money market fund.

BOND TRADING SIGNALS

A summary of all moving average signals that required action while trading the Fidelity High Income Bond Fund

Date	Signal
4/ 9/80	Buy signal—both indices cross above their moving averages. Buy shares of the High Income Bond Fund with all available capital on 4/10 at 7.97 per share. Stop-loss point = 7.81.
4/16/80	NAV of fund = 8.17, cancel stop-loss point.
7/29/80	Sell signal—both indices cross below their moving averages. Sell all shares of the fund on 7/30 at 8.60 per share.
12/26/80	Buy signal—buy shares on 12/29 at 7.96. Stop-loss point = 7.80.
2/13/81	Sell signal—NAV of fund = 7.77, below the stop-loss point. Sell all shares on 2/16 at 7.76.
3/17/81	Buy signal—buy shares on 3/18 at 7.94. Stop-loss point = 7.78.
4/ 9/81	Sell signal—NAV of fund = 7.77, below the stop-loss point. Sell all shares on 4/10 at 7.76.
5/27/81	Buy signal—buy shares on 5/28 at 7.63. Stop-loss point = 7.48.
6/15/81	NAV of fund = 7.80, cancel stop-loss point.
7/ 2/81	Sell signal—both indices cross below their moving averages. Sell all shares on 7/6 at 7.70 per share.
10/12/81	Buy signal—buy shares on 10/13 at 7.00. Stop-loss point = 6.86.

BOND TRADING SIGNALS (Cont'd)

Date	Signal
11/ 6/81	NAV of fund = 7.20, cancel stop-loss point.
12/14/81	Sell signal—both indices cross below their moving averages. Sell all shares on 12/15 at 7.38 per share.
1/29/82	Buy signal—buy shares on 2/1 at 7.07. Stop-loss point = 6.93.
5/12/82	NAV of fund = 7.22, cancel stop-loss point.
6/ 4/82	Sell signal—both indices cross below their moving averages. Sell all shares on 6/7 at 7.15 per share.
7/12/82	Buy signal—buy shares on 7/13 at 7.09. Stop-loss point = 6.95.
8/ 2/82	NAV of fund = 7.27, cancel stop-loss point.
5/23/83	Sell signal—both indices cross below their moving averages. Sell all shares on 5/24 at 9.09 per share.
8/24/83	Buy signal—buy shares on 8/25 at 8.79. Stop-loss point = 8.61.
9/26/83	NAV of fund = 8.97, cancel stop-loss point.
10/26/83	Sell signal—both indices cross below their moving averages. Sell all shares on 10/27 at 9.02 per share.
1/ 3/84	Buy signal—buy shares on 1/6 at 8.97. Stop-loss point = 8.79.
3/13/84	Sell signal—NAV of fund = 8.78, below the stop-loss point. Sell all shares on 3/14 at 8.79.
7/13/84	Buy signal—buy shares on 7/16 at 8.10. Stop-loss point = 7.94.
8/ 2/84	NAV = 8.29, cancel stop-loss point.
12/31/84	End test period. NAV = 8.59.

TRADING RESULTS

Having developed each of the trading signals, we can now

examine the results that would have been obtained if we had acted on each signal. It is assumed that the program was started with capital of $10,000 and that all interest and capital gains were reinvested in the appropriate fund at the end of each month. It should be noted that, in the bond trading system, our capital is always earning interest—either in the money market fund or in the bond fund. Therefore, the interest earned on our capital is a very important aspect of the trading program.

The $10,000 starting capital was placed in the Fidelity Cash Reserves Fund on January 1, 1980. On each bond buy signal, the cash in the money market fund was exchanged to the Fidelity High Income Bond Fund on the day following the signal. On each sell signal, all the bond funds were sold and the proceeds were exchanged back to the Cash Reserves Fund, again on the day after the signal.

The following table gives the results of each of the 10 round-trip trades and the cumulative trading results over the entire test period.

TRADING RESULTS
Fidelity High Income Bond Fund

Cycle	Capital	Interest	Buy Price	Sell Price	Proceeds	Capital Gain	Capital
1	$10,000	$ 840	7.97	8.60	$11,195	$ 820	$11,660
2	11,660	835	7.96	7.76	11,943	– 308	12,187
3	12,187	254	7.94	7.76	12,047	– 279	12,162
4	12,162	445	7.63	7.70	12,515	114	12,721
5	12,721	911	7.00	7.38	13,964	719	14,351
6	14,351	1,146	7.07	7.15	14,823	166	15,663
7	15,663	2,523	7.09	9.09	20,320	4,471	22,657
8	22,657	1,024	8.79	9.02	23,783	606	24,287
9	24,287	1,016	8.97	8.79	24,213	– 496	24,807
10	24,807	2,574	8.10	8.59	27,204	1,552	28,933

Total Gain   = $18,933   Percent Gain   = 189.3%

Percent/Year   =   37.9%   Compounded   =   23.7%

Time period - 5 Years

APPENDICES

APPENDIX A

The Twenty-Seven Trading Cycles of the New York Stock Exchange

STOCK MARKET CYCLES
NYSE Index and Date at Various Points of Each Trading Cycle

Cycle	Market High	First Buy Signal	Market Low	Sell Plan	Market High	Sell Signal
1	5/13/65 48.50	6/28/65 43.64	6/28/65 43.64	9/ 3/65 47.26	11/15/65 49.65	12/ 6/65 48.92
2	2/ 9/66 51.06	5/13/66 46.09	10/ 7/66 39.37	10/27/66 43.15	5/ 8/67 51.93	5/24/67 49.85
3	1/12/68 54.17	2/13/68 49.72	3/ 5/68 48.70	4/ 3/68 51.48	7/11/68 57.69	7/22/68 55.81
4	5/14/69 59.32	6/19/69 54.01	7/29/69 49.31	10/16/69 53.76	11/10/69 55.12	11/19/69 53.63
5	11/10/69 55.12	1/28/70 48.59	5/26/70 37.69	8/21/70 42.85	4/28/70 57.76	5/17/71 55.48
6	4/28/71 57.76	7/29/71 53.06	8/ 9/71 51.66	8/17/71 55.27	9/ 8/71 56.04	9/22/71 54.27
7	9/ 8/71 56.04	10/20/71 52.85	11/23/71 49.60	12/ 3/71 53.51	4/12/72 61.42	4/25/72 59.75
8	1/11/73 65.48	2/ 7/73 61.37	7/ 6/73 53.36	7/20/73 57.09	7/26/73 58.54	8/ 7/73 56.29
9	7/26/73 58.54	8/20/73 54.19	8/22/73 53.55	9/19/73 56.90	10/12/73 60.25	11/ 1/73 57.94
10	10/12/73 60.25	11/12/73 55.96	2/11/74 48.57	3/ 5/74 52.17	3/13/74 55.37	3/27/74 51.59
11	3/13/74 53.37	4/24/74 47.96	10/ 3/74 32.89	10/14/74 38.36	10/14/74 38.36	10/16/74 37.12
12	11/11/74 39.77	12/ 5/74 35.08	12/ 6/74 34.45	1/ 3/75 37.35	7/15/75 51.24	7/23/75 48.40
13	7/15/75 51.24	7/29/75 47.20	9/16/75 43.59	10/ 9/75 46.72	10/23/75 48.25	11/ 3/75 46.56
14	9/21/76 57.51	10/12/76 53.87	11/10/76 52.90	12/ 8/76 55.93	12/31/76 57.88	1/12/77 55.95

STOCK MARKET CYCLES
(Cont'd)

Cycle	Market High	First Buy Signal	Market Low	Sell Plan	Market High	Sell Signal
15	12/31/76 57.88	10/12/77 51.22	10/25/77 49.86	11/11/77 52.70	11/25/77 53.33	12/ 6/77 51.33
16	11/25/77 53.33	1/ 9/78 55.05	3/ 6/78 48.37	4/14/78 51.94	9/11/78 60.38	9/19/78 57.84
17	9/11/78 60.38	10/19/78 55.71	11/14/78 51.36	1/ 5/79 55.41	1/26/79 56.99	2/ 5/79 55.01
18	10/ 5/79 63.39	10/12/79 59.29	10/25/79 56.61	11/26/79 60.91	12/17/79 62.61	1/ 2/80 60.69
19	2/13/80 67.77	3/ 7/80 60.96	3/27/80 55.30	5/19/80 61.39	10/15/80 77.24	10/30/80 72.85
20	11/28/80 81.02	12/10/80 73.78	12/11/80 73.11	12/22/80 77.94	1/ 6/81 79.14	1/ 8/81 76.20
21	1/ 6/81 79.14	2/ 2/81 72.67	2/20/81 72.45	3/13/81 76.32	3/25/81 78.82	4/29/81 76.84
22	3/25/81 78.82	7/ 6/81 73.99	7/22/81 73.90	8/11/81 77.65	8/11/81 77.65	8/18/81 75.55
23	8/11/81 77.65	8/24/81 72.92	9/25/81 64.96	11/ 2/81 72.05	11/ 4/81 72.38	11/16/81 69.99
24	11/30/81 73.37	1/13/82 66.63	3/ 8/82 62.02	4/ 8/82 66.89	5/11/82 68.80	5/18/82 66.84
25	5/11/82 68.80	6/17/82 61.96	8/12/82 58.80	8/20/82 64.65	6/22/83 99.01	7/15/83 95.28
26	6/22/83 99.01	8/ 8/83 92.19	8/ 8/83 92.19	9/ 6/83 96.84	10/10/83 99.63	10/19/83 96.16
27	1/ 6/84 97.71	2/ 8/84 90.09	7/24/84 85.13	8/ 2/84 90.77	11/ 6/84 98.12	11/16/84 94.70

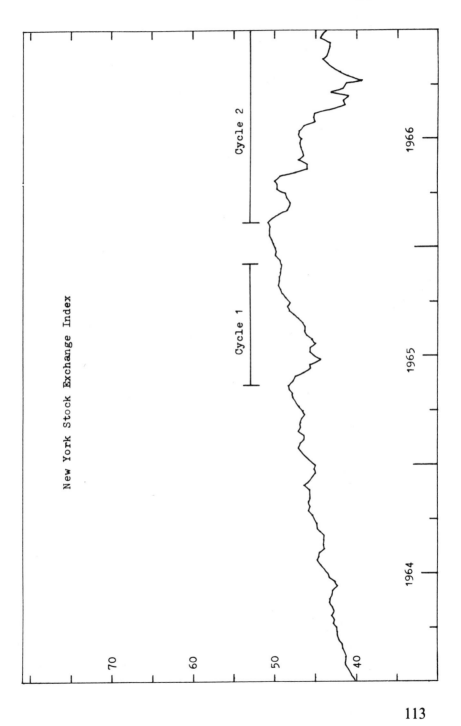

Appendix A

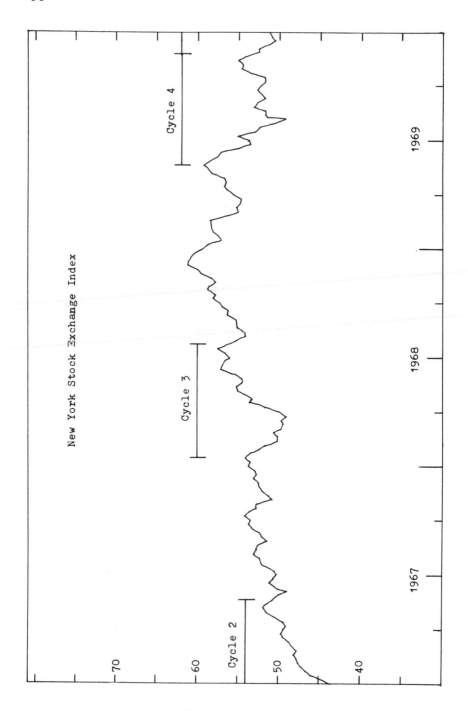

114

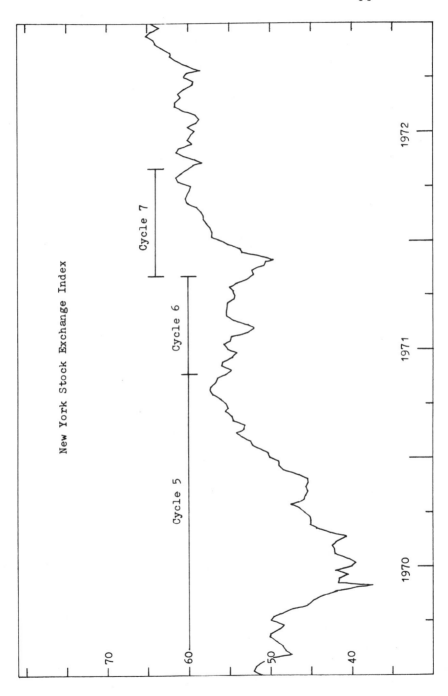

New York Stock Exchange Index

Appendix A

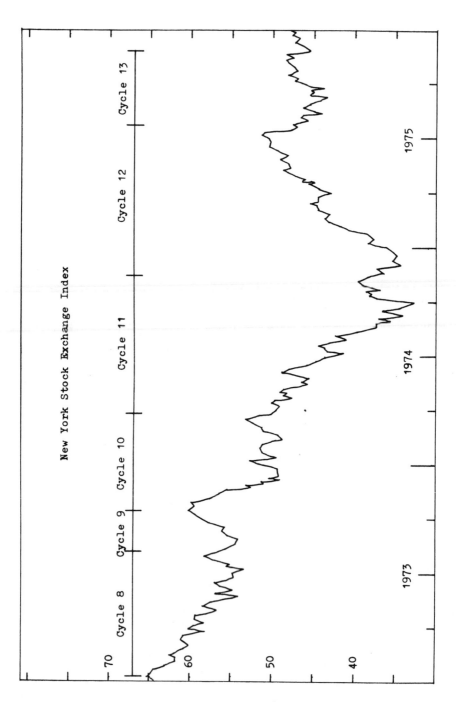

116

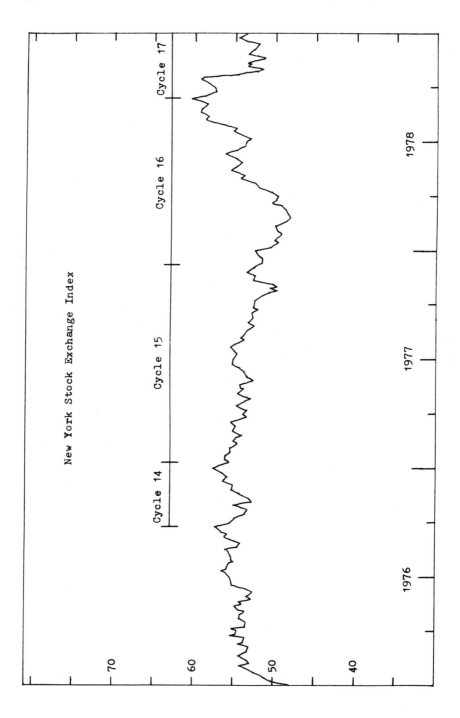

Appendix A

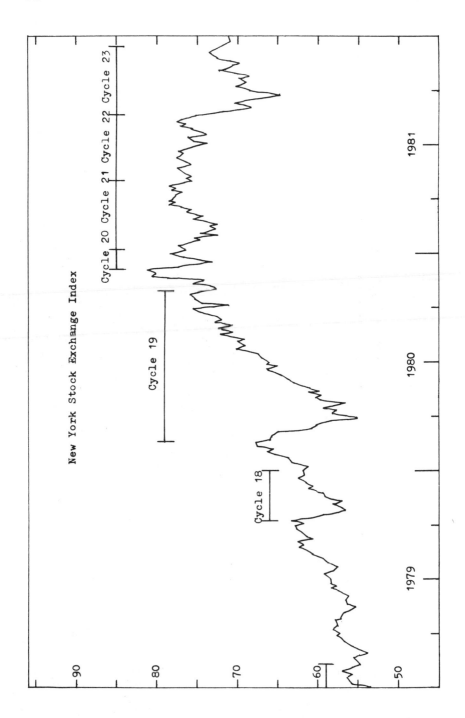

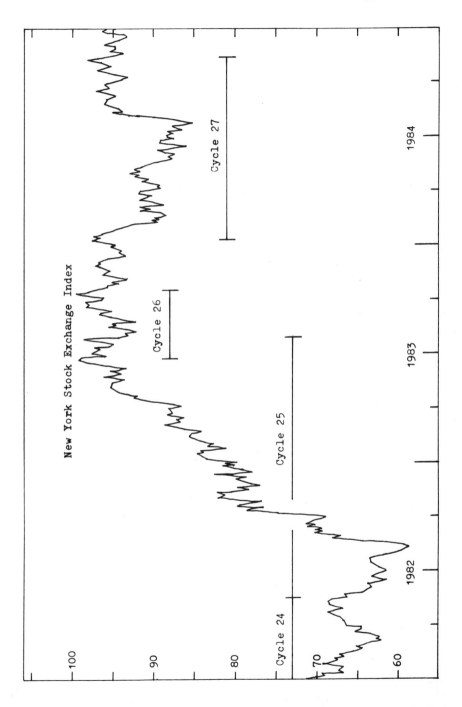

APPENDIX B

**Trading Signals Developed By The
New York Stock Exchange Index
Between June, 1965 and December, 1984**

TRADING SYSTEM FOR THE NYSE INDEX
All Buy and Sell Signals Developed By The System
For The NYSE Index

Date	Index	Oscillator	Signal	Invest
6/28/65	43.64	− 6.00	Buy 1	$1,000
9/ 3/65	47.26	+ 2.16	MA Buy-Sell	
			Plan	100%
12/ 6/65	48.92	− 0.13	Sell	100%
5/13/66	46.09	− 5.37	Buy 1	1,000
8/ 1/66	44.60	− 4.29	Buy 2	40%
8/19/66	43.21	− 5.57	Buy 3	40%
8/26/66	41.41	− 8.22	Buy 4-Bear	
			Signal	100%
8/29/66	40.32	− 10.25	Safety Sell	100%
10/ 7/66	39.37	− 7.47	Buy 1	1,000
10/27/66	43.15	+ 2.10	Sell Plan	
12/12/66	44.93	+ 3.58	MA Buy	100%
5/24/67	49.85	− 0.75	Sell	100%
2/13/68	49.72	− 5.08	Buy 1	1,000
4/ 3/68	51.84	+ 2.58	MA Buy-Sell	
			Plan	100%
7/22/68	55.81	− 0.10	Sell	100%
6/19/69	54.01	− 5.01	Buy 1	1,000
7/14/69	52.37	− 5.47	Buy 2	40%
7/28/69	49.73	− 8.33	Buy 3	40%
10/16/69	53.76	+ 2.43	Sell Plan	
10/21/69	54.31	+ 3.14	MA Buy	100%
11/19/69	53.63	− 0.15	Sell	100%
1/28/70	48.59	− 5.15	Buy 1	1,000
4/22/70	46.47	− 5.07	Buy 2	40%
4/24/70	45.53	− 6.50	Buy 3	40%
4/28/70	44.08	− 8.84	Buy 4	100%
5/12/70	42.73	− 8.72	Safety Sell	100%
5/14/70	41.37	− 10.86	Buy 1	1,000
5/21/70	39.46	− 13.11	Buy 2	40%

TRADING SYSTEM FOR THE NYSE INDEX
(Cont'd)

Date	Index	Oscillator	Signal	Invest
5/25/70	38.20	− 14.91	Buy 3	40%
5/25/70	37.69	− 15.51	Buy 4	100%
8/21/70	42.85	+ 2.81	Sell Plan	
9/ 4/70	45.11	+ 6.01	Bull Signal	
11/16/70	45.30	− 0.13	Set Stop-Sell	
11/27/70	46.64	+ 2.60	Rally	
5/17/71	55.48	− 0.84	Sell	100%
7/29/71	53.06	− 3.53	Buy 1	1,000
8/17/71	55.27	+ 2.16	MA Buy-Sell Plan	100%
9/22/71	54.27	− 0.80	Sell	100%
10/20/71	52.85	− 3.09	Buy 1	1,000
11/11/71	50.87	− 4.58	Buy 2	40%
12/ 3/71	53.51	+ 2.15	MA Buy-Sell Plan	100%
4/25/72	59.75	− 0.13	Sell	100%
2/ 7/73	61.37	− 3.12	Buy 1	1,000
3/21/73	59.07	− 4.12	Buy 2	40%
4/27/73	56.86	− 4.86	Buy 3	40%
5/18/73	54.96	− 6.19	Buy 4	100%
7/20/73	57.09	+ 2.23	Sell Plan	
8/ 7/73	56.29	− 0.31	Sell	100%
8/20/73	54.19	− 3.32	Buy 1	1,000
9/19/73	56.90	+ 2.11	Sell Plan	
9/21/73	57.73	+ 3.33	MA Buy	100%
11/ 1/73	57.94	− 0.32	Sell	100%
11/12/73	55.96	− 3.15	Buy 1	1,000
11/19/73	53.76	− 6.09	Buy 2	40%
11/26/73	51.51	− 9.90	Buy 3- Bear Signal	40%
12/13/73	50.08	− 9.87	Buy 4	40%
3/ 5/74	52.17	+ 2.20	Sell Plan	
3/27/74	51.59	− 0.23	Sell	100%

TRADING SYSTEM FOR THE NYSE INDEX
(Cont'd)

Date	Index	Oscillator	Signal	Invest
4/24/74	47.96	− 5.13	Buy 1	$1,000
5/20/74	46.36	− 5.73	Buy 2	40%
6/28/74	44.90	− 5.54	Buy 3	40%
7/ 5/74	43.60	− 7.25	Buy 4	100%
7/ 8/74	42.25	− 9.76	Safety Sell	100%
8/ 2/74	41.17	− 7.86	Buy 1	1,000
8/16/74	39.76	− 7.86	Buy 2	40%
8/21/74	38.59	− 10.38	Buy 3	40%
8/23/74	37.55	− 11.97	Buy 4	100%
9/ 4/74	35.93	− 12.89	Safety Sell	100%
9/12/74	34.88	− 13.14	Buy 1	1,000
9/30/74	33.45	− 12.27	Buy 2	40%
10/14/74	38.36	+ 3.09	Sell Plan	
10/17/74	37.52	− 0.28	Sell	100%
12/ 5/74	35.08	− 6.05	Buy 1	1,000
1/ 3/75	37.35	+ 2.54	Sell Plan	
1/27/75	40.12	+ 7.54	Bull Signal	
1/28/75	40.43	+ 8.01	MA Buy	100%
4/ 7/75	42.69	− 0.02	Set Stop-Sell	
4/ 9/75	43.88	+ 2.63	Rally	
7/23/75	48.40	− 1.36	Sell	100%
7/29/75	47.20	− 3.40	Buy 1	1,000
8/19/75	45.23	− 5.06	Buy 2	40%
9/16/75	43.59	− 5.60	Buy 3	40%
10/ 9/75	46.72	+ 2.10	MA Buy-Sell Plan	100%
11/ 3/75	46.56	− 0.02	Sell	100%
10/12/76	53.87	− 3.08	Buy 1	1,000
12/ 8/76	55.93	+ 2.14	MA Buy-Sell Plan	100%
1/12/77	55.95	− 0.10	Sell	100%

TRADING SYSTEM FOR THE NYSE INDEX
(Cont'd)

Date	Index	Oscillator	Signal	Invest
10/12/77	51.22	− 3.09	Buy 1	$1,000
11/11/77	52.70	+ 2.01	Sell Plan	
11/27/77	53.33	+ 2.57	MA Buy	100%
12/ 6/77	51.33	− 1.38	Sell	100%
1/ 9/78	50.05	− 3.34	Buy 1	1,000
4/14/78	51.94	+ 3.89	MA Buy-Sell Plan	100%
4/25/78	53.81	+ 6.12	Bull Signal	
6/21/78	53.91	− 0.40	Set Stop-Sell	
7/25/78	55.27	+ 2.01	Rally	
9/19/78	57.84	− 0.05	Sell	100%
10/19/78	55.71	− 3.67	Buy 1	1,000
10/26/78	53.48	− 6.48	Buy 2	40%
10/31/78	51.67	− 8.74	Buy 3-Bear Signal	
1/ 5/79	55.41	+ 2.44	MA Buy-Sell Plan	100%
2/ 5/79	55.01	− 0.31	Sell	100%
10/19/79	57.62	− 5.01	Buy 1	1,000
11/26/79	60.91	+ 2.86	MA Buy	100%
1/ 2/80	60.69	− 0.12	Sell	100%
2/ 8/80	67.57	+ 6.31	Bull Signal	
3/ 6/80	61.94	− 3.75	Buy 1	1,000
3/17/80	58.22	− 8.08	Buy 2-Bear Signal	40%
3/24/80	56.47	− 9.51	Buy 3	40%
3/27/80	55.30	− 10.30	Buy 4	100%
5/19/80	61.39	+ 2.12	Sell Plan	
6/10/80	65.43	+ 6.00	Bull Signal	
9/29/80	71.26	− 0.32	Set Stop-Sell	
10/ 1/80	73.37	+ 2.47	Rally	
10/30/80	72.85	− 1.11	Sell	100%

TRADING SYSTEM FOR THE NYSE INDEX
(Cont'd)

Date	Index	Oscillator	Signal	Invest
12/10/80	73.78	− 3.45	Buy 1	$1,000
12/22/80	77.94	+ 2.29	MA Buy-	
			Sell Plan	100%
1/ 8/81	76.20	− 0.78	Sell	100%
2/ 2/81	72.67	− 4.45	Buy 1	1,000
3/13/81	77.19	+ 2.94	MA Buy-	
			Sell Plan	100%
4/29/81	76.84	− 0.05	Sell	100%
7/ 6/81	73.99	− 3.28	Buy 1	1,000
8/11/81	77.65	+ 2.22	MA Buy-	
			Sell Plan	100%
8/18/81	75.55	− 0.72	Sell	100%
8/24/81	72.92	− 3.94	Buy 1	1,000
9/ 3/81	70.25	− 5.96	Buy 2	40%
9/ 8/81	68.24	− 8.09	Bear Signal	
9/17/81	67.83	− 7.05	Buy 3	40%
9/25/81	64.96	− 9.29	Buy 4	100%
11/ 2/81	72.05	+ 2.69	Sell Plan	
11/16/81	69.99	− 0.85	Sell	100%
1/13/82	66.63	− 5.60	Buy 1	1,000
2/22/82	64.55	− 4.98	Buy 2	40%
3/ 8/82	62.03	− 7.02	Buy 3	40%
4/ 8/82	66.89	+ 2.03	Sell Plan	
5/18/82	66.84	− 0.22	Sell	100%
6/17/82	61.96	− 5.02	Buy 1	1,000
8/20/82	64.65	+ 3.67	Sell Plan	
8/23/82	66.36	+ 6.14	MA Buy	100%
8/23/82	66.36	+ 6.14	Bull Signal	
1/24/83	80.92	− 0.16	Set Stop-Sell	
1/27/83	83.17	+ 2.44	Rally	
7/15/83	95.28	− 0.20	Sell	100%
8/ 8/83	92.19	− 3.34	Buy 1	1,000
9/ 6/83	96.84	+ 2.08	MA Buy-	
			Sell Plan	100%
10/19/83	96.16	− 0.52	Sell	100%

127

TRADING SYSTEM FOR THE NYSE INDEX
(Cont'd)

Date	Index	Oscillator	Signal	Invest
2/ 6/84	91.43	− 4.04	Buy 1	$1,000
5/23/84	88.09	− 3.14	Buy 2	40%
7/24/84	85.13	− 3.41	Buy 3	40%
8/ 2/84	90.77	+ 3.18	MA Buy-	
			Sell Plan	100%
8/ 9/84	94.97	+ 6.69	Bull Signal	
10/ 3/84	93.74	− 0.39	Set Stop-Sell	
10/18/84	96.81	+ 2.67	Rally	
11/16/84	94.70	− 0.77	Sell	100%

APPENDIX C

Trading Results For The
New York Stock Exchange Index
Between
June, 1965 and December, 1984

TRADING RESULTS
New York Stock Exchange Index

Trade Cycle	Start Capital	Average Buy Price	Sale Price	Sale Proceeds	Gain	New Capital
1	$10,000	47.05	49.38	$10,496	$ 496	$10,496
2	10,496	43.31	40.99	9,933	− 563	9,933
2A	9,933	44.28	50.34	11,292	1,359	11,292
3	11,292	51.91	55.70	12,116	824	12,116
4	12,116	51.36	53.04	12,511	395	12,511
5	12,511	45.41	41.99	11,569	− 942	11,569
5A	11,569	38.96	55.52	16,488	4,919	16,488
6	16,488	54.42	54.37	16,472	− 16	16,472
7	16,472	52.24	59.62	18,799	2,327	18,799
8	18,799	57.11	56.30	18,534	− 265	18,534
9	18,534	57.67	57.61	18,513	− 21	18,513
10	18,513	51.71	50.63	18,126	− 387	18,126
11	18,126	45.18	42.40	17,009	− 1,117	17,009
11A	17,009	38.71	37.04	16,276	− 733	16,276
11B	16,276	33.48	37.52	8,416	906	17,181
12	17,181	40.58	48.27	20,437	3,256	20,437
13	20,437	44.54	46.78	21,464	1,027	21,464
14	21,464	56.13	56.39	21,564	100	21,564
15	21,564	52.93	51.28	20,889	− 675	20,889
16	20,889	52.54	57.32	22,787	1,898	22,787
17	22,787	53.53	54.99	23,407	620	23,407
18	23,407	60.59	60.34	23,309	− 98	23,308
19	23,308	57.64	73.53	29,736	6,428	29,736
20	29,736	77.48	76.44	29,336	− 400	29,336
21	29,336	76.69	76.81	29,381	45	29,381
22	29,381	77.31	75.73	28,779	− 602	28,779
23	28,779	68.20	70.39	29,705	926	29,705
24	29,705	63.69	66.32	25,785	1,021	30,726
25	30,726	63.04	94.96	46,284	15,558	46,284
26	46,284	96.86	96.32	46,026	− 258	46,026
27	46,026	87.56	94.10	49,462	3,436	49,462

Total Gain $39,463   Percent Gain 394.6%
Percent/Year 20.2%   Compounded 8.5%
Time - 19.5 Years

Note: A and B after cycle number indicate further trading within the same cycle after safety sell singals.

APPENDIX D

Momentum Charts For The New York Stock Exchange Index And The OTC Composite Index

Appendix D

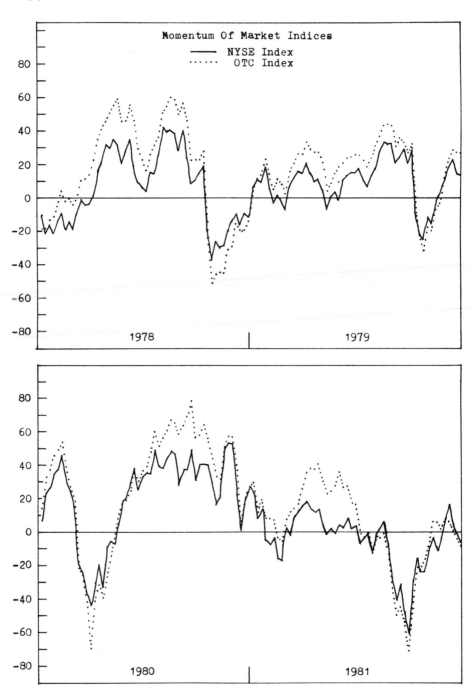

134

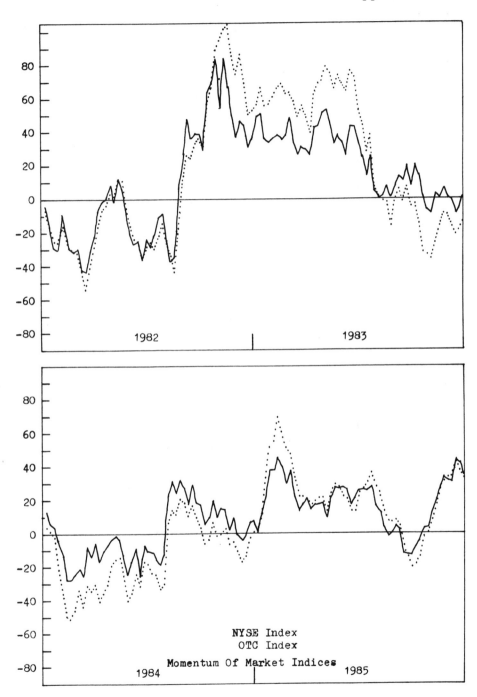

NYSE Index
OTC Index

Momentum Of Market Indices

APPENDIX E

Charts of the United Services Gold Shares Fund Net Asset Value With 15-Day And 200-Day Moving Averages

Appendix E

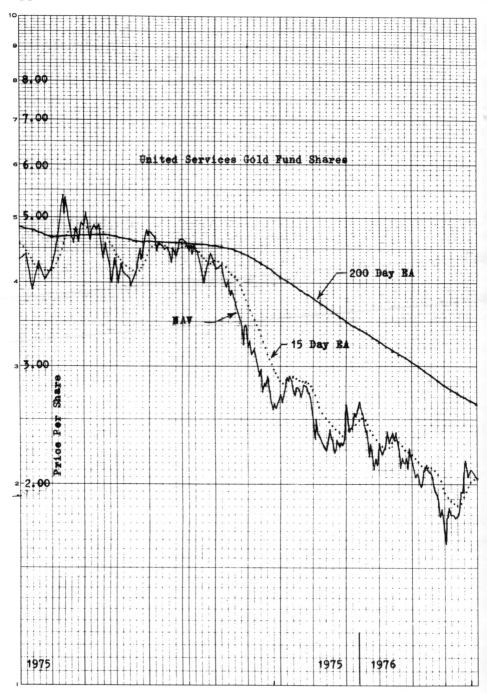

138

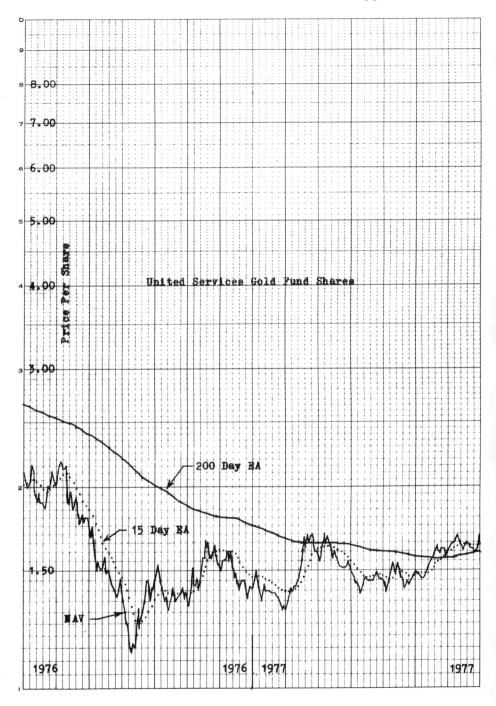

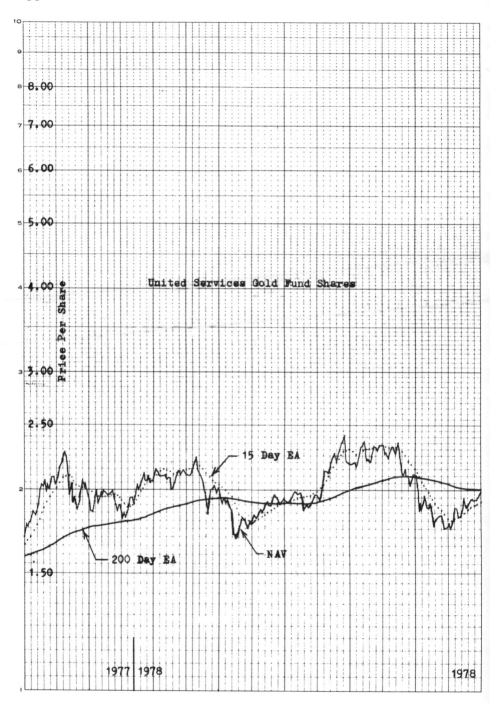

United Services Gold Fund Shares

15 Day EA

200 Day EA

NAV

1977 | 1978

1978

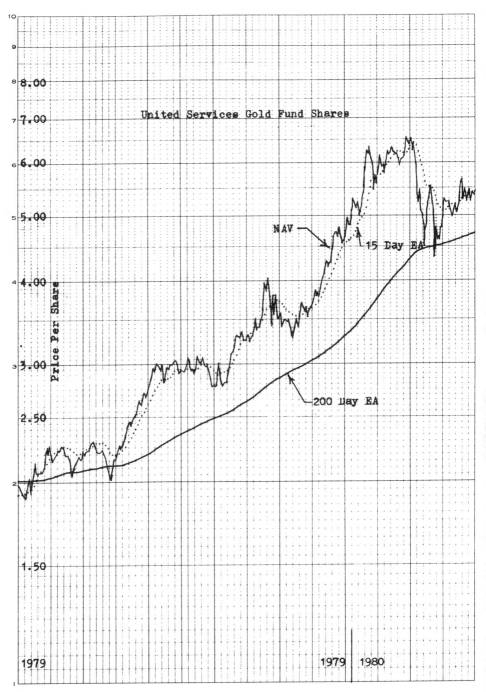

Appendix E

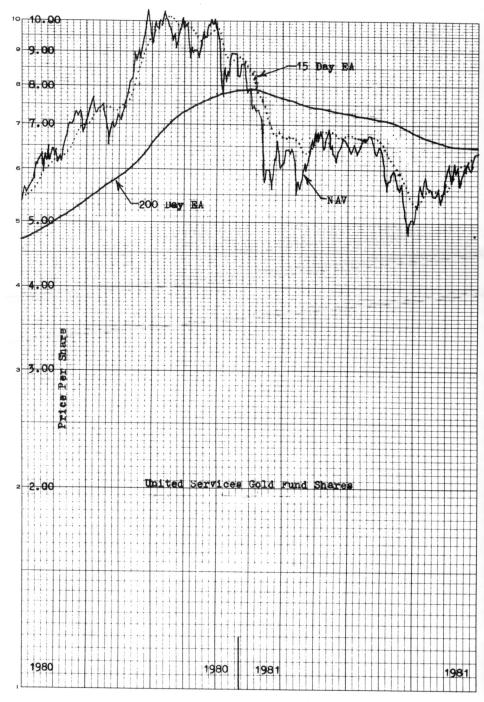

United Services Gold Fund Shares

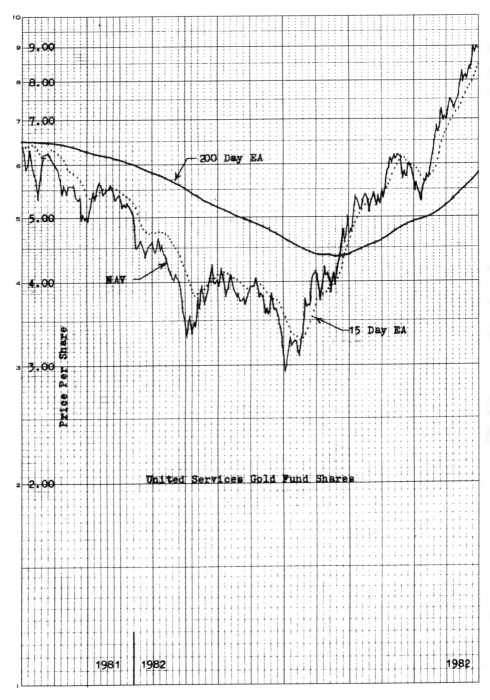

United Services Gold Fund Shares

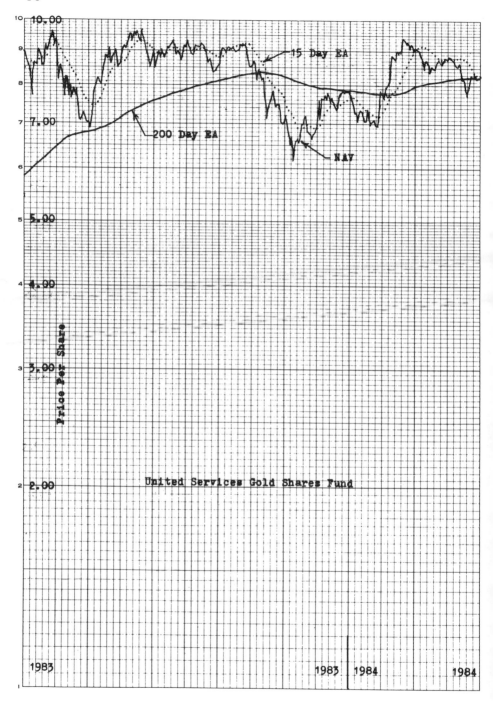

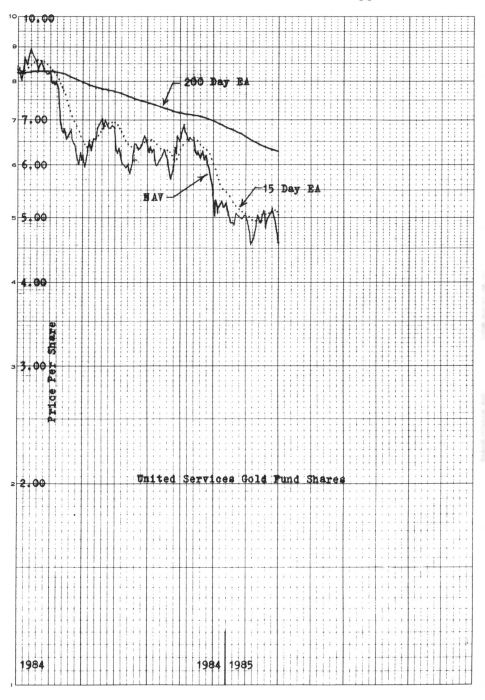

APPENDIX F
Market Update

The development of the trading techniques for no-load mutual funds was completed using market data through the end of 1984. It now seems appropriate to examine how the system has continued to work since the end of 1984. The following tables list all of the trading signals that have been generated since the last signal listed in the text, as well as the trading results that have been obtained by acting on those signals.

TRADING SIGNALS FOR STOCK MUTUAL FUNDS

A Summary of all Oscillator and NYSE Index Signals That Required Some Action While Trading No-Load Mutual Funds Since 1984

Date	Signal
11/16/84	Oscillator declines to −0.77, sell signal. Sell all shares.
9/17/85	Oscillator = −3.50, NYSE Index = 104.89. Buy signal, purchase shares of the fund with $1,000. Next buy point = 101.22, a 3½% decline in the index.
11/ 1/85	NYSE Index = 110.55, 39-week EA = 106.23, Oscillator = +2.40. This is a moving average buy signal. Buy shares with all remaining capital. Sell plan in effect.
12/13/85	NYSE Index = 120.83, oscillator = +6.32 - major bull market signal. Bull market sell plan in effect.
1/22/86	NYSE Index = 117.75, oscillator = −0.13 - caution signal. Calculate stop-loss sell point that is 2% below the NAV of each fund held. Sell if the fund closes below that point.
1/28/86	NYSE Index = 121.10, oscillator = +2.49. Market rally - cancel stop-loss sell points and sell all shares when the oscillator next declines to 0.

149

TRADING RESULTS FOR SOME STOCK FUNDS
SINCE 1984

Trade Cycle	Invest	Average Price	Last NAV	Market Value	Capital Gain	Interest	Percent Gain
Constellation Growth Fund							
12	$10,640	20.97	24.85	$13,946	$3,391	$ 640	39.5%
Stein Roe Capital Opportunities Fund							
12	10,640	20.81	25.53	13,051	2,411	640	30.5%
Stein Roe Special Fund							
12	10,640	15.86	19.14	12,841	2,201	640	28.4%
Stein Roe Discovery Fund							
12	10,640	9.65	12.54	13,825	3,185	640	38.2%
Boston Capital Appreciation Fund							
12	10,640	26.07	31.41	12,820	2,180	640	28.2%
Boston Special Growth Fund							
12	10,640	17.33	21.24	13,043	2,403	640	30.4%

TRADING SIGNALS FOR
UNITED SERVICES GOLD SHARES FUND
A Summary of All Signals That Required Some Action
While Trading the United Services Gold Shares Fund
Since 1984

Date	Signal
6/27/84	NAV = 7.90, 15-day EA = 8.243, 200-day EA = 8.267. Moving average sell signal. Sell all shares.
12/28/84	NAV = 5.26, 15-day EA = 5.457, 200-day EA = 6.830. 15-day EA is 20.1% below the 200-day EA. Buy signal—purchase shares of the fund with 20% of capital. Next buy point = 4.21, a 20% decline in the NAV of the fund.
1/24/85	Dividend = .15, next buy point = 4.06.
4/16/85	NAV = 5.66, 15-day EA = 6.033, 200-day EA = 6.049. Moving average buy signal. Purchase shares of the fund with all available capital.
5/ 1/85	NAV = 5.66, 15-day EA = 6.033, 200-day EA = 6.049. Moving average sell signal. Sell all shares.
8/27/85	NAV = 4.03, 15-day EA = 4.386, 200-day EA = 5.495. 15-day EA is 20.2% below the 200-day EA. Buy signal—purchase shares with 20% of capital. Next buy point = 3.22.
9/27/85	Dividend = .12, next buy point = 3.10.
11/ 4/85	NAV = 2.96, buy shares with 20% of starting capital. Next buy point = 2.48.
1/30/86	NAV = 4.65, 15-day EA = 4.536, 200-day EA = 4.524. Moving average buy signal. Buy shares with all available capital.
2/ 7/86	Dividend = .14, NAV = 4.35.
2/21/86	NAV = 4.66.

TRADING RESULTS FOR
UNITED SERVICES GOLD SHARES
DINCE 1984

Trade Cycle	Invest	Buy Price	Sell Price	Market Value	Capital Gain	Interest	New Capital
9	$10,191	5.96	5.63	$ 9,625	− $ 566	$ 191	$ 9,625
10	$10,075	3.97	4.66	11,829	1,754	450	11,829

Note: $10,000 grows to $11,829 for an 18.3% gain in 14 months.

TRADING SIGNALS FOR BONDS

A Summary of All Moving Average Signals that Required Action While Trading the Fidelity High Income Bond Fund Since the July 13, 1984 Buy Signal.

Date	Signal
7/13/84	Buy signal—both indices cross above their moving averages. Buy shares of the High Income Bond Fund with all available capital on 7/16 at 8.10 per share. Stop-loss sell point = 7.94.
8/ 2/84	NAV = 8.29, cancel stop-loss point.
2/25/85	Sell signal—both indices cross below their moving averages. Sell all shares on 2/26 at 8.80.
3/29/85	Buy signal—buy shares of the fund on 4/1 at 8.77 per share. Stop-loss sell point = 8.59.
5/14/85	NAV = 8.96, cancel stop-loss sell point.
7/26/85	Sell signal—sell all shares on 7/29 at 9.16.
8/19/85	Buy signal—buy shares of the fund on 8/20 at 9.19 per share. Stop-loss sell point = 9.00.
12/13/85	NAV = 9.39, cancel stop-loss sell point.
1/27/86	Dividend = .13, NAV = 9.28.
2/21/86	NAV = 9.49.

TRADING RESULTS FOR
FIDELITY HIGH INCOME BOND FUND
SINCE 1984

Trade Cycle	Invest	Interest	Buy Price	Sell Price	Proceeds	Capital Gain	New Capital
10	$10,000	$ 993	8.10	8.80	$11,789	$ 881	$11,874
11	11,874	574	8.77	9.16	12,925	532	12,980
12	12,980	854	9.19	9.49	14,545	711	14,545

Note: $10,000 grows to $14,545 for a gain of 45.5% in 19 months or 27%/year.